THE ULTIMATE CYBER SECURITY GUIDE

CONQUER

THE

WEB

Edited by Jonathan Reuvid

Legend Business Ltd, 107-111 Fleet Street, London, EC4A 2AB
info@legend-paperbooks.co.uk | www.legendpress.co.uk

Print ISBN 9781787198623
Set in Times. Printing managed by Jellyfish Solutions Ltd
Cover design by Tom Sanderson | www.the-parish.com/

Publishers Note
Every possible effort has been made to ensure that the information contained in
this book is accurate at the time of going to press, and the publishers and authors
cannot accept responsibility for any errors or omissions, however caused. No
responsibility for loss or damage occasioned to any person acting, or refraining
from action, as a result of the material in this publication can be accepted by the
editor, the publisher or any of the authors.

CONTENTS

INTRODUCTION

Take a moment to imagine what it feels like to fall victim of a cyber-attack, to suddenly find your hard-won reputation and livelihood in peril.

Jim Baines, the main character in the AXELOS Global Best Practice novel, *Whaling for Beginners*, is a fictional representative of practically every real world small business leader.

Jim values his business, a highly successful and respected packaging firm. He is driven, innovative and values transparency, as do many small business owners and entrepreneurs. But in one sense, Jim is complacent. He casually clicks on a malevolent email attachment and, as a consequence, his business, and those of his customers and associates, are threatened.

To Jim's credit, he is brave enough to write an open letter to his peers about his experiences. It's an emotional plea, a call to action to other small business leaders to better understand, plan for, and respond to the cyber-risks that endanger their organisation's hard-won reputation, competitive advantage and operational capabilities. It's a plea to be resilient as they grow and mature their businesses.

There's a very real chance this scenario could happen to you. In the *Small Business Guide*, the National Cyber

Security Centre reports that "there's a 1 in 2 chance that you'll experience a cyber security breach"[1]. Research by Barclays Business Banking[2] shows that over 10% of SME businesses have suffered a cyber-attack, with almost 9% making staff redundant to cover the cost of cybercrime.

Resilience to cyber-attacks is still not a critical priority for most individuals or SME owners. The Centre for Economics and Business Research[3] notes that, alongside cashflow and rising costs, businesses are more concerned with finding talented new staff than with preparing for unforeseen circumstances in an increasingly chaotic and fast-moving world.

However, there are simple, practical, low-cost steps that you or your business can take to become more resilient and vigilant in the face of escalating cyber-attacks. You don't need to be a technical wizard. You don't need to make massive financial investments. But you need to appreciate that you will be attacked at some point, and you need to understand where your greatest vulnerabilities lie, namely our own human frailties and capacity for error. Managing cyber risk should be 'business as usual', just as with every other business or personal risk.

The hackers share stories about us. They say we're too slow, flawed and myopic to see through their schemes, and too staid to keep up with their tricks. But we're not. We can resist and fight back. But only if we understand what's ultimately at stake – human livelihoods and reputations – and provided we change our ways to protect ourselves.

---

1. https://www.ncsc.gov.uk/content/files/protected_files/guidance_files/cyber_security_small_business_guide_1.2.pdf

2. See: https://realbusiness.co.uk/tech-and-innovation/2018/04/30/left-unchecked-cyber-criminals-will-squeeze-life-small-firms

3. See: http://www.bmmagazine.co.uk/news/investing-staff-number-one-priority-smes/

We need more stories like Jim's to demonstrate the dangers of waiting until it's too late. We need more real world cyber stories from the frontline, talking about resilience in the wider context of the priorities that face small, medium and global firms.

I'm delighted to write this introduction. Books like these are essential reading, contending with the ceaseless threat to our livelihoods by utilising shared knowledge, vigilance, and resilience.

Nick Wilding
General Manager, Cyber Resilience,
AXELOS Global Best Practice

Read more about Jim Baines:
https://www.axelos.com/resilia/whaling-for-beginners

PART ONE

DAY TO DAY LIVING IN THE CYBER WORLD

by

Tim Mitchell
Content Director of Get Safe Online

1.1

PROTECT YOUR COMPUTER AND DEVICES

There's a commonly-quoted statistic in law enforcement and information security circles: 80% of cyber-dependent and cyber-enabled crimes could be avoided if we all just changed our behaviours and took more care when using the internet.

It could be argued that 'behaviours' and 'taking more care' mean knowing when not to click on links or attachments in emails, nor paying someone you don't know by bank transfer, or donating to charity only via well-known channels (and many, many others). And that protecting your computer, smartphone or tablet is about technology, not your online behaviour. However, the ongoing and very necessary task of *making sure that these devices are protected* constitutes a behaviour in its own right, so don't blame the tech if you become a victim of fraud because your antivirus runs out, because it's your responsibility to make sure it doesn't.

To many, this will sound like common sense, but one of the most common flaws in human nature is putting things off.

The last things I want are for you to stop using the internet, and for you to become paranoid (or to think *I'm* paranoid). But cyber-enabled and cyber-dependent crimes are the fastest-growing of any, and I'd like to think that you will read and heed the advice and make being careful the default when going online and using your devices.

MALWARE

Viruses, spyware and other malware (malicious software) represent big business for the cybercriminal fraternity, whether they're devising and coding new strains, selling it on to other criminals, hosting it, distributing it and generally profiting from the dishonest gains made at the expense of their victims. Malware can cause many things to happen, from generating clicks in order to artificially boost advertising revenue, making your device part of a 'botnet' to swamp a website with traffic in order to close it down (known as a Distributed Denial of Service or DDoS attack). Some can snoop on all your online transactions including email, banking and payments; some can even activate your webcam to quite literally spy on you or your family.

Then there's ransomware, which is when criminals literally hold you to ransom by locking access to your files and programs until a financial ransom is paid (allegedly). Ransomware is one of the most burgeoning and insidious threats today and has become well-known owing to a number of high-profile and damaging attacks.

Malware is one of those terms which started off in a technical sector (cybersecurity / information security in this case) and has subsequently been adopted by everyone. Having said that, some internet users still aren't aware of the term, instead still using 'viruses' as a catch-all, which technically, isn't accurate. So let's define the word malware, and stick with it.

Putting it simply, malware is <u>malicious software</u> coded with the intent of causing harm to a user, a system, or a network. It can at best disrupt and, at worst, cripple its targets in a number of ways, depending on its nature and objectives. It is programmed to act by stealth, often residing on devices and systems for long periods of time while the user (you or I) remain oblivious. It is usually disguised as a clean program. For consumers, the effects of a malware infection can range from inconvenience to, literally, financial ruin. For organisations, add business interruption, loss of revenue, reputation damage and possibly closure. There's a well-documented incident regarding a senior executive in a business who plugged his vaping charger (albeit a spurious model not supplied with the original kit) into his company computer, only to be informed by the IT department that it had been pre-loaded with malware, which proceeded to infect not only his device ... but the entire network.

Malware has been around for many years ... the term was coined in 1990 but viruses had already been around for decades. Given that its development and distribution is a multi-million-pound industry (for criminals), it's not surprising that it evolves at an alarming rate and, to be frank, the cybersecurity industry and law enforcement struggle to keep up with it when it comes to protection. It's often quoted that over a million new malware threats are released *every day*. It's hard to conceive the scale of this and the havoc it wreaks amongst ordinary computer and mobile device users in their personal and business lives. This is why the *combination* of the best malware protection you can afford – and understanding what you can do to avoid the issues that can cause you problems – are so vital.

Types of malware

I have no wish to get overly technical, but in a book on cybersecurity I think it's important to discuss the different types of malware out there, give you a brief explanation of what they do, and what this means for you if you're affected. These are listed in no particular order.

Viruses
To be described as a virus, malware must be able to reproduce the code that's programmed into it, meaning that it will distribute copies of itself by any means possible. It will infect a device or network but work away in the background undetected, hiding within files whilst the device executes (runs) the code. A virus generally needs some kind of human intervention to propagate, such as you clicking on an infected attachment or visiting a malicious website.

There are three main types of virus:

1. *File infectors*
    An 'executable file' on a computer is one that is used to perform a task, rather than one that contains data like a word processing document or photo. Some viruses enter ordinary executable files (such as those with a .EXE or .COM extension) by stealth, in readiness for that function to be instigated by the user. Batch and script files such as those with .BAT, .JS. and .VB extensions are also susceptible, as well as screensaver (.SCR) files.

2. *System / boot infectors*
    Some viruses are designed to infect your computer by installing themselves as part of its operating system, residing in the RAM (random

access memory). Nowadays, security built into contemporary operating systems has largely combated these types of viruses, so cybercriminals are less likely to develop and distribute them. However, this does indicate the importance of you running the latest version of the operating system that your device will allow.

3.   *Macro viruses*
     Macro viruses run inside certain software applications that allow macro programs to offer more functions. They can result in accessing sensitive information, data theft and consuming system resources, often explaining a noticeable deterioration in the performance of infected systems, such as slow running, overheating and the inability to perform the most basic tasks. Macro viruses used to be renowned for targeting Microsoft Office programs, but these days unsigned macros are automatically disabled.

Worms

Worms are small, standalone programs that replicate without targeting specific files apart from the operating system files, indiscriminately destroying files and data on the device until the drive that they're inhabiting is empty. Unlike viruses, which latch on to existing files, worms are self-contained.

Worms generally arrive via emails and instant messages, exploiting security vulnerabilities to spread via networks. Some worms are designed to merely use computers and networks to spread, rather than damaging them, but this doesn't make them any less malicious.

Trojans

A Trojan horse is named after the legendary wooden horse disguised by the ancient Greeks as an offering to Athena – but actually concealed around 40 soldiers who opened the gates of Troy, leading to its downfall. Normally referred to simply as a 'Trojan' this malicious program misrepresents itself as authentic software to appear genuine and convince you, the PC user, to install it on your device. Not unlike what happened in Troy, some types of modern-day Trojans disguise themselves as software that removes viruses, whereas they are doing precisely the opposite: installing them.

Trojans can carry (and disguise) pretty much anything, but generally they're items of malware that create a 'backdoor' that enables criminal access to your computer. Critically, they enable access to your personal information: passwords, banking details and IP addresses to name but a few. Some can snoop on your keystrokes to harvest logins and payment card data. Many ransomware attacks are also perpetrated by Trojans.

Spyware

As the name suggests, spyware is a kind of malware designed to constantly spy on you or, more accurately, spy on what you're doing on your connected device. It can take many different forms ... from tracking your internet activity in order to exploit your interests for commercial gain to downloading adware, to gathering information about you without your knowledge, again from your online activity but also from data you have stored. This could include financial or other personal information in order to perpetrate various types of fraud, identity theft or both. It could also include your photos, videos and sound recordings.

One kind of spyware that is becoming more common-place is a Remote Access Trojan or, appropriately, RAT, for short. RATs are usually downloaded without your knowledge, with a program legitimately requested by you such as a game, or perhaps as an email attachment.

Obtaining your confidential information or capturing your every financial transaction is bad enough. However, a particularly insidious application for RATs is to activate your webcam or other internet-connected cameras around the home or office, and therefore, quite literally, spy on you. The motives are varied – from facilitating webcam blackmail (such as threatening to post footage of what you're doing sitting at your computer), to financial or identity fraud, or just for kicks. Cases that come to mind are an 18 year old student who was watching a video on her laptop whilst in the bath and spotted that the LED next to the built-in webcam was illuminated, and a Russian website that broadcast an array of feeds from many cameras around the world that it had activated via spyware infections. You should note that some variants don't activate the LED – just the camera – so you may not even know that you're being watched.

In addition to the advice I always give about avoiding malware by having up-to-date antivirus installed and not clicking on spurious links or attachments, I also advise you to cover up your webcam if you're worried about being physically spied on. You can buy an inexpensive device for this, but to my mind, a Post-it or piece of opaque adhesive tape is ample.

Ransomware
Ransomware has actually been in existence since the late 1980s, rose to prominence in 2013 and almost became a household name in 2017 with the 'WannaCry'

attack, which infected more than 300,000 computers in 150 countries. In the UK alone, more than 80 National Health Service hospitals were impacted, resulting in cancelled surgeries and diverted ambulances. But it can just as easily affect individuals' own computers or, increasingly, mobile devices.

Many regard ransomware as the most malicious type of ransomware, as it blocks access to your data, accompanied by a screen which demands a ransom, normally payable in digital currency. Sometimes, it 'merely' locks your system, difficult enough for most people to remedy. More sophisticated versions, however, actually encrypt your files, rendering them inaccessible until the ransom is paid. Restoration is best left to an expert and therefore normally not cheap. Sometimes, the perpetrators also threaten to publish your data online.

However, there's no guarantee that paying the ransom will restore your access to the data nor prevent it from being deleted. I advise you to never even consider making a ransom payment if this happens to you.

Good day-to-day online practice on your part will help to prevent a ransomware attack. It should go without saying that your computer should be protected by an updated antivirus program. Cybercriminals also look for security weaknesses in your software – including your operating system – so it's essential to update all software when prompted, as updates almost invariably contain security patches. Better still, set software and operating systems to update automatically, then you won't have to worry about it.

Be careful about the websites you visit, as some are found to be infected (either intentionally or inadvertently), which could in turn cause an infection on your own device.

The existence and effects of ransomware also serve to reinforce the importance of performing regular backups of all or selected important data. It's perfectly possible that you'll lose financial records, important documents or cherished photos altogether in a ransomware attack, with the consequences ranging from inconvenience to heartache. Businesses who have failed to back up their data can suffer revenue losses, reputational damage, financial penalties and even closure.

Keyloggers

A keylogger is a type of software program that records (logs) all the information that you type on your keyboard and sends it to the cybercriminal who has installed it on your computer. It runs in the background, so you're unaware that your keystrokes are being monitored.

In this way, the perpetrator can obtain sensitive information such as usernames, passwords and payment card details. From continuous monitoring over a number of transactions, it is even possible to obtain the memorable information requested along with the password … set up when you opened the account. Keyloggers do not have the capability to record information typed on virtual keyboards.

Adware

Considered to be one of the most lucrative (for its distributors) but least harmful types of malware, adware (short for 'advertising-supported software') is designed specifically to display advertisements on your computer, or certain types of mobile device, as pop-ups. For its distributors, it earns revenue in two ways: by the act of displaying the advertisement, and by charging the advertiser for each occasion it is clicked (known as 'pay-per-click').

To you, it could be presented as a static or moving box or banner, a full screen display or a video, with or without sound. Whilst adware is not generally regarded as a threat, but rather more an irritation, most commercial antivirus programs can detect and block it.

How does your device get infected by malware?

The writing, sales and distribution of malware is a massive growth industry, and as in all successful business sectors, those involved will exploit as many channels and delivery methods as possible.

Via attachments
A favourite way for cybercriminals to infect your device with malware is via bogus attachments, which can be disguised as documents, photos, exe. or other files. Clicking on the attachment to open it, can cause malware to directly download on to your device, or enable ongoing online communication with a 'command and control' server. Spyware, ransomware, adware and many other types of malware can be introduced this way, as well as recruiting your device to become part of a botnet, mobilised to cause financial and reputational damage to targeted websites without your even being aware of it.

Via links
Malicious links can be found in 'phishing' emails, 'smshing' text messages and 'twishing' social media posts or messages. Typically, they are designed to exploit human nature, such as the desire to avoid problems, get a great deal on a purchase or take advantage of a free offer.

The original type of scam emails, some of which are still being distributed – and unfortunately still responded to – are known in law enforcement and cybersecurity circles as '419' scams, named after Article 419 of the Nigeria's criminal code, concerning fraud. The senders claim to have come into considerable sums of money, some of which they want to gift you, normally in return for an advance fee. These days, scam communications have become far more sophisticated. emails can include your name (as if from an authorised organisation such as your bank, the tax authorities or law enforcement), they can feature authentic-looking branding and they can even appear to come from an authorised email account, thanks to address spoofing. Fraudulent text messages and social media posts can be equally deceptive.

Inevitably, the link in any of these communications leads to a bogus, but normally convincing website, which will either (1) request you to fill in confidential financial or other personal details which the fraudster can use to defraud you of your money or identity, or both, or (2) cause your device to be infected with malware. The key advice here is to type in the address that you know to be correct into your browser, rather than simply clicking on links in unsolicited or unexpected communications. It may take a little longer, but better to be safe than sorry.

Via infected websites
It's perfectly feasible – and this happens frequently – to inadvertently download malware from visiting infected websites. They may be infected accidentally, without the knowledge of the owner or hosting company, or they may be set up specifically as a facilitator to committing fraud or ID theft, or both. In

the cybersecurity business, these are often known as 'drive-by downloads'.

Some of the most commonplace types of malicious site are those designed to closely emulate authentic sites with lots of traffic such as an online retailer, utility company or government department. They're so convincing that security experts struggle to tell the hoax site from the original.

A favourite ploy of cybercriminals is to subtly change the website address or URL – even by one letter – to fool you into thinking it's the original. Fraudulent websites may, as outlined in 'via links' above, request your personal information, but are equally likely to infect your device with some kind of malware. I repeat, it's safer to type in the address you know to be authentic, and always check for spelling accuracy.

Some kinds of websites are notorious for being the source of malware infections. Adult sites are a case in point. Authentic adult site operators are just as keen as retailers, government departments or utilities to keep their sites 'clean' of malware, after all, they have revenues and reputations to protect like any other business. However, the nature of adult surfing activity – often supported by the affiliate business model – lends itself to users moving from one site to another, and even if the original, reputable site is unaffected by malware, it's possible that clicking on one of the many links will result in visiting a malware-riddled site.

At a public event I was working at, a gentleman approached me clutching his laptop, asking what could be done to rid his device of the ransomware which had locked access to all his files. It transpired that he frequented pornographic sites with no regard to the links he was clicking on and hey presto, up popped

CryptoLocker, despite his laptop having the latest, paid-for antivirus protection. He was in for an expensive time if he wanted his access back.

Via USB/disk
If you found a USB memory stick (a.k.a. pen drive, flash drive) lying around, would your natural curiosity lead you to plug it into your computer to find out what it contained? Possibly, but even more so if somebody actually handed or sent you the memory stick, telling you its contents would be of interest in either your work or personal life.

Chances are that the storage device is perfectly innocent, but then again, this is a well-known method of distributing malware. Even a work colleague or family member may inadvertently pass on an infected USB stick.

The same goes for other USB-connected storage devices (such as portable hard drives) as well as cameras, mobile phones and anything else you can plug in. Remember the vaping CEO, mentioned previously? And, though not in use so much these days thanks to cloud and network-attached storage and the bandwidth and speed to effortlessly transfer large files online, CDs and DVDs can also deliberately or inadvertently be used to spread malware.

Smartphones and tablets, too, can acquire malware via aftermarket chargers and powerpacks not supplied with the original device. I'm not saying this is going to happen to you, but it *could*.

Virus protection on your computer

From time to time, I participate at events, advising the general public and small businesses how to stay safe online. It still never fails to amaze me how many people – and even small businesses – don't have up-to-date – if indeed any – active antivirus protection on their computers. The subject comes up either when I routinely ask if they have activated protection in response to a question regarding a computer that is riddled with issues or why fraud or identity theft has occurred.

Why, exactly, don't people have effective antivirus on their computers?

"It'll never happen to me"
As in many aspects of life, some people seem to think that they're cocooned in some kind of protective bubble which will save them from everyday hazards like being run down whilst cycling in the dark without lights, crossing the road without looking … or using their computer without malware protection. I don't know the relative probabilities, but I'll bet that people come unstuck more often as a result of the last one.

"I thought it was protected"
All new PCs (desktops and laptops) are pre-loaded at the factory with internet security programs from the manufacturer's choice of vendor. All you need to do is register your details with the vendor, and you're up and running. You *must* remember that if you don't register your details to activate the program, you can still go online, but you're not protected.

And, of course, the security vendor isn't supplying that software to the computer manufacturer through altruism, but because they want you to pay to renew the licence after the initial free trial period, sticking with their software because it's prevented any issues and it's easier than loading or downloading an alternative product. You will receive ample warning that the validity of the security program is about to expire and that you need to renew the licence in order to avoid malware infections. If you don't do this – or install an alternative product – again your device won't be protected.

Further down the line, your antivirus program will still inform you every time the licence is about to expire. This should be sufficient to prompt you into renewing it, but if not, you can specify automatic renewal as it falls due (normally annually), or simply make a diary entry to renew manually.

"My computer doesn't need it"
Because in online security not everything is cut-and-dried, I'm going to refute this notion, then qualify it. If you're a PC owner, if all you want to do is to defend your computer against viruses, spyware and other malware, you have a degree of inbuilt protection with Microsoft's own Windows Defender (or in Windows versions before 8, Windows Security Essentials). It does not offer some of the sophisticated add-on features of specialists' programs but makes no apology for that.

Again, however, you need to ensure that Windows Defender is switched on, and set up to update automatically. As a caveat, this built-in solution sometimes doesn't perform well in independent lab comparison tests, so you may want to consider alternatives.

However, the main group of people who will tell you that their computers don't need malware protection are Apple users. This used to be largely true, owing to the Apple's technical architecture coupled with the fact that the relatively small population of Apple machines (compared with PCs) made it unprofitable for criminals to develop and spread specific malware. Nowadays, however, as the proportion of Macs increases and because their owners tend to have more money, making them a more financially attractive target, we hear of an increasing number of successful malware attacks, making *"My computer doesn't need it"* a myth.

Virus protection on your mobile devices

We've established that having malware protection on your computer is one of the central pillars of online safety. But what about your mobile devices?

The latter part of 2016 saw the balance change to more users accessing the internet from mobile devices than from desktops or laptops. So why aren't the mobiles the subject of malware infections too?

The simple answer is: they are.

This increasing use, coupled with better security on computers, has made your mobile device – whether a smartphone or tablet – the *Number One target* for malware attacks by cybercriminals. Plus, in a way, it is easier to infect a mobile device with malware because you have less control over the environment you use them in. Many people also tend to lower their guard when using mobile devices … *"It's just a phone".* Actually, it's also a computer, camera, satnav, wallet, games console and much, much more. Why *wouldn't* it be a prime target for malware?

Phones and tablets with the Android operating system – even the latest versions – are particularly susceptible to malware, to the degree that having malware protection should be as natural as having it on your computer.

What antivirus protection should you use

Having established that malware is a major cause of fraud, identity theft and attacks on third-party systems, let's take a look at how to protect your device against becoming infected.

There are many antivirus programs for computers – and apps for your mobile devices – on the market. They vary considerably, certainly in functionality and sophistication but more importantly, effectiveness … and cost.

If I recommend, or even name, the suppliers that come to mind instantly, I'd be in danger of excluding some very good ones, or maybe not being impartial. Therefore, as a rule of thumb, the well-known, reputable, global suppliers all offer ranges of products which offer the best-available protection for your device. I say 'best available' for a very good reason: nothing is foolproof. However good the antivirus and however much you pay for it, it is not 100% guaranteed to prevent issues. Echoing what I wrote previously about online behaviour, *you* are the third element of the holy trinity of protection, along with your antivirus and the device itself.

Any antivirus software you choose should, by definition, have the basics when it comes to safeguarding your device: blocking incoming malware, and the provision of scheduled and on-demand scans.

Others have additional or enhanced features which you may or may not want. I'd recommend products with more features, given the wide variety of threats that your connected devices have to deal with every day. You would expect the feature-loaded products to cost more, but frequently, they do not. Some of the additional features you may find are specific spyware and ransomware protection, firewalls, backups, malicious URL blocking, phishing email detection, vulnerability scans and even behaviour-based detection. Go online, read reviews and comparisons on reputable websites and make your own mind up.

Protection for mobile devices comes in the form of an app, of which there are many reputable products available, again varying considerably in functionality and cost. As with computer antivirus protection, read reviews and make up your mind which product is the best for you, taking into account added features. Some include parental controls, some have trackers to help locate your phone or tablet in the event of loss or theft, some even take a selfie of the first person to attempt unlock it using the wrong code, and email you the picture along with their GPS location, without their knowledge. This is sometimes accompanied by remote backup, restore or data wipe. There are a lot of product variants, so it pays to take time checking exactly what you're getting, before you buy.

Paid-for or free?

As a rule of thumb, protecting your devices with free programs or apps is like having a standard lock on the front door of your home. They're 'adequate' in that they provide a degree of protection and are better than nothing. Paid-for products are generally preferable in that they (1) are updated more frequently to provide better protection against the tsunami of new malicious programmes developed and distributed every day (hundreds of thousands), (2) offer you customer service and technical support in the event of user issues, and (3) are generally the subject of continuous added features and improved protection. To continue the analogy, paid-for products represent the deadlocks and alarm systems of your devices. Many antivirus products are provided free as a hook to draw you into buying the paid-for version.

Buying and installing antivirus

Whilst many antivirus products are still sold for stand-alone, one-device protection, many are now bundled so that you can load them on to multiple devices – including Apple computers, phones and tablets – providing ease of use and the comfort of familiarity with how they work and look. You can buy online or in-store, and nowadays installation is usually by entering a code, which you get when you've paid, entering it on the manufacturer's website and following the normally very clear downloading instructions.

As previously mentioned, choose whether you want the software/app to renew automatically at the end of the first twelve-month licence period. Doing so will give you peace of mind that your protection will continue uninterrupted, but it does mean that you need to make sure you remember that renewal will happen automatically, and that you have the money in your bank account when it's debited.

One other important point: do not have two antivirus programs installed at the same time as they will cancel each other out and your device won't be protected.

UPDATES

Why do we have updates?

One of the most important rules of online safety is that when you receive a prompt to update operating systems and applications on your computer and your mobile devices, *just do it*.

When creating and distributing malware, cybercriminals seek out the fastest and easiest route to load it on to your devices. Earlier in this chapter, we discussed how the human element represents the biggest threat, and that includes not taking care of the tech. Not installing updates is a prime example.

Software and app updates frequently incorporate improvements to usability and look and feel, and often contain new features. Ambivalent about any of these, a lot of people don't heed the prompt to download them. Either because they're not tech-savvy, hold the view 'if it ain't broke don't fix it – or they'll 'get around to it later'.

However – and I'm not just saying this because I'm in the security business – by far the most important reason you *must* download updates, is that they frequently contain security fixes – often referred to as patches or service packs. In effect, if you don't do so, the software is indeed, 'broke'. The most reputable and widely-used operating systems and software – Microsoft, Apple and Adobe included – contain vulnerabilities which it is the career cybercriminal's mission to exploit. An expert coder with criminal intent and the promise of rich rewards can seek out these Achilles Heels and infiltrate your device with the objective of infecting it with malware. Device and software manufacturers employ huge security teams looking for cracks in their products' armour, and developers to fix them, by producing and distributing patches. They even pay a bounty to individuals who uncover these vulnerabilities ... it's worth it to protect their users and their reputation.

Having previously spoken about how even the best and most up-to-date antivirus products are fallible, and hundreds of thousands of new strains of malware are invented every day, the importance of updating operating systems, software programs and apps cannot be overstated.

How updates work

On your computer, you'll generally be notified about updates by pop-up message or a new icon in your system tray. Users of the Windows operating system and other Microsoft software will be familiar with 'patch Tuesday' – when the company releases its routine updates on the second Tuesday of each month (this is when you're warned not to power down your computer until they have been applied to it). When a vulnerability is discovered, software vendors will frequently release emergency patches and urge you to apply them there and then.

You are given the option of managing some software updates on your computer automatically, which I strongly recommend to give you peace of mind. Operating system, antivirus and some other software can be configured to automatically download and install updates for you. If you're unable to find this automatic update option in your software, look at the manufacturer's support pages on their website, or contact them via their helpline or online enquiry form.

Somewhat confusingly, not all software offers automatic updates. Adobe® Reader® and Java, for example, provide a small icon in the system tray at the bottom of your screen, which you need to click to set the update process in motion.

Mobile phones and tablets also have their operating systems and apps updated frequently, and it's equally important that you apply these to remain as secure as possible. Click on your device's app store icon and you'll find a list of apps which require you to update them, and those which have updated automatically. You'll often see a list of improvements, and these are often connected with removing vulnerabilities or fixing bugs.

Updates are installed over the current installation and don't need you to uninstall or re-install the operating system, software or app in question. The updater will do what it has to do, quietly and efficiently.

Updates v upgrades

Many people confuse the term 'update' with 'upgrade', but they are completely different. As explained above, an update downloads the fixes and improvements to update your operating system, program or app to the current version, but doesn't upgrade it to the next version. An upgrade, however, allows you to move up to the next major version, for example Windows 8.1 to 10, or Apple OS X Mountain Lion to macOS High Sierra.

Updates are normally downloaded at no cost to the user … they are included in the original or annual software licence, whereas you'll have to pay for an upgrade.

BACKUPS

The importance of backing up

This is another topic of which I can't overstate the importance: backing up your files is vital. For those of us (and that's most people) who have come to rely on digital technology for many aspects of our lives, things which used to take up physical space are now stored electronically. Sure, filing cabinets, photo albums, CDs, DVDs and written or typed letters still exist, but they're fast being consigned to history as digital creation and storage take over. They've been replaced by computers and mobile devices, which offer increasing storage capacity and – in the case of computers – decreased costs.

There is, however, a massive down-side to relying purely on your devices for storing these items (apart from the fact that they may be accessible to people whom you don't want to see them), and that's the possibility of losing it in the event of loss, theft, damage, malfunction or inadvertent deletion. Not only that, but as the incidence of ransomware increases, so does the risk of data loss, with your files effectively locked and potentially, never accessible again. Making backups is much easier and far cheaper than trying to recover files from a hard drive that has been compromised in this way, and, of course, it's perfectly common for computer hard drives to break down.

The answer is to have effective, reliable storage in place ... and to make sure you use it. There are a number of different ways to back up the data from your computer; with mobile devices it's a more straightforward process.

Backing up your computer

Making copies of your files – whether documents, photos, music or video – is essential if you don't want to lose them in one of the ways described above. However, at the risk of stating the obvious, it's very important that the copies aren't kept in the same place. If your portable hard drive containing all of your backed-up data is kept next to your computer and there's a flood, fire or theft, there's a fair chance that both will be destroyed.

There are several options to choose from when it

comes to backing up your computer. Whichever you choose, it is far easier to use a method which performs incremental backups (automatically detects and saves updates and additions), rather than the laborious task of manually backing up, deleting, replacing or re-naming old versions of files.

Cloud backups
Cloud backup is the easiest kind to create and maintain. With the ongoing decrease in the cost of online storage, you can also get a lot of storage for a surprisingly low cost.

All you need to do is to select a cloud storage vendor to suit your needs, create an account, download their software on to your computer, run it to log in and register your account information and set your preferences. It's pretty much that simple, as the software will automatically back up your files all the time your computer is turned on and online. Once the initial backup is complete, the software detects only differences, and uploads only the data which is new or has been updated.

At this point, I should recommend that before you select a vendor, do some research. What are the relative costs? Is the vendor set up for your kind of usage (are you looking at one that's more aligned with large corporate customers, when you need only 'normal' personal use)? How secure is it? How easily and quickly will you be able to retrieve your backed-up files when you need them? What guarantees do you have? You'll find this information easily online in computing magazine and other independent reviews. Talk to friends and family about their own experience of backups.

Most cloud backups work in roughly the same way: your files are encrypted for security purposes, and then copied to multiple drives – normally in different physical locations – so that there's no single point of failure and your data will be safe in the event of technical faults or natural occurrences such as fires or floods.

Initial upload speeds tend to be slow, and you may wonder if your data is, in fact, being transferred. However, your control panel will indicate the amount of data backed up, including as a proportion of the total. Checking this from time to time will give you the confidence that the backup is running quietly and reliably in the background. Depending on the volume of data you're backing up and the speed of your internet connection, it could take days or even weeks, but when it's backing up lots of small files in a sequence, it's great watching the 'remaining files' number whizzing to an ever-decreasing number, hundreds at a time.

External hard drive backups
An alternative, and more traditional way to create an archive of your changed and deleted files to by using an external hard drive to create an archive of your changed and deleted files.

Most of today's external hard drives to be used on PCs include their own software which performs incremental backups (in common with cloud services). External hard drives are generally used only to back up personal data such as photos, which would be irreplaceable if your computer were lost, damaged, developed a malfunction or was locked with ransomware. If you use apply the archive functionality of this type of backup, and the files on your computer hard drive are updated or deleted, you can use the backup to undo the updates and recover the deleted files. You can also plug it into another computer in the event that the original one fails to work.

Unlike cloud storage – which offers virtually unlimited storage (for a price) – the amount of data you can store on an external hard drive is limited by its capacity. The size of the drive will also restrict how far you can go back in time to retrieve deleted and earlier versions of files, as older updates may have been nudged out by the other data that you're backing up. You also need to bear in mind that being an item of electro-mechanical equipment, an external hard drive will wear out and, subsequently, fail to work, with the possible consequence of rendering your backed-up data irrecoverable. A friend of mine has resisted backing up his data to the cloud (I suspect for reasons of cost), but instead continues to back up his data to his ten-year old external hard drive … probably a recipe for disaster. In some cases, it's possible to retrieve the data and save it to a new drive using specialist knowledge. However, this isn't cheap, and I suspect my friend is guilty of false economy.

If you're a Mac user wishing to backup data to an external hard drive, you have the option of using Time Machine, an application bundled with your Apple operating system. Time Machine runs every hour, checking for changes and performing incremental hourly backups for the previous 24 hours, daily backups for the previous month and weekly backups for previous months until the space on the external hard drive is exhausted. As is the case with PC backup software, it then deletes the oldest weekly backups in deference to newly backed-up data. As an option, you can invest in Time Capsule, which handles Time Machine backups over Wi-Fi. Ideally – and this is often not feasible owing to the fact that the external hard drive generally remains physically connected to your computer via USB port – your backup should be stored in a separate place from the computer to safeguard it against physical damage or theft. This serves to highlight why cloud backup is a safer option.

USB flash (pen) drives

Flash drives are an easy way to save files for use elsewhere when not connected to a network, or email is unavailable or inappropriate. They may also be used to back-up your data, but owing to their relatively very limited storage capacity, they are generally unsuitable (and therefore not recommended) for this purpose, especially considering the large file sizes of data such as photos, videos and music files.

Being of small physical size – a benefit when it comes to portability and sharing – flash drives can also easily lost, 'put down somewhere' or stolen, which makes your backed-up data not only unavailable, but also potentially accessible to others.

Backing up your mobile devices

Setting up backups on your smartphone or tablet is a considerably more intuitive process than on your computer. It is easily done in your device's settings, where, provided you have the cloud storage associated with your device's operating system (such as iCloud or Google Cloud Platform) set up, you can set it to automatically back up every day.

There are a also a number of third-party cloud backup services available to smartphone and tablet users, including Dropbox, Google Drive and those from some device manufacturers.

1.2

USING SMARTPHONES AND TABLETS

It wasn't until 2007 that Apple introduced the iPhone and Microsoft the Windows Mobile, with Google's Android G1 phone following the year after. In 2010, the first tablets were launched by Apple and Samsung respectively. 2011 saw smartphones outsell personal computers for the first time, and two years later, tablets outsold laptops for the first time. The concept of the smartphone had been around a little longer, however, as in 1992 IBM had developed a prototype mobile phone that incorporated features from a PDA (personal digital assistant) – itself a popular concept back in the day incorporating a diary and address book. The first commercially-available model was produced and sold by IBM and BellSouth in the US in 1994, called the Simon Personal Communicator. The ensuing years saw further advances in technology by several manufacturers until those landmark introductions in the late noughties.

Why the history lesson? To demonstrate that in a very short space of time, we have witnessed in the development of mobile devices, astonishing progress in technology and equally astonishing speed in how it has been adopted ... not by scientists or astronauts, but by *all of us*. Processing power and storage that used to demand whole buildings can now fit into the palm of your hand.

I often hear people ask, either literally or rhetorically, "how did we manage before?". Has technology evolved to suit us, or have we changed our behaviours to align our lives with the fact that it's become so readily available? I'd say that both are the case. We're hungry for things that make our lives easier and deliver benefits faster, so yes, technology is constantly evolving to suit us. However, before mobile phones we couldn't live or work somewhere without a landline in case our kids had a fall in the playground and the school needed to get hold of us, nor text directions to a friend.

Nowadays, of course, we rely on our mobile devices for much, much more than these relatively mundane tasks thanks to advances in processing power, availability of ever increasing bandwidth and the spectacular (and, some would say bewildering) array of apps available on all mobile platforms. We can see if we'll need to get up 15 minutes early the next morning to scrape the ice off the windscreen, or check traffic conditions en route to a meeting (having pulled over first, of course). We can check the news, follow our favourite box set, watch (and gamble on) the big game, book flights and do our banking ... all from a park bench. We can control our lights, heating controls and security systems and even check the contents of our refrigerator from the other side of the world. It seems there's little we *can't* do from our smartphone or tablet, which is, in reality, a computer, a camera, a photo album, a filing cabinet, a GPS, a TV, a jukebox, a wallet, and much more.

Take a step back and you'll realise that our reliance on our mobile devices, and in particular our smart-phones, is astonishing. For more than 50% of us, checking our phone is the first thing we do after waking in the morning. For many, it's also the last thing we do at night. I swear that in not too many generations' time, mankind will have evolved to have a hand that resembles a mobile phone holder.

The technology, our reliance on it and what it enables, make it crucial that you protect your mobile devices in every meaning of the word in order to safeguard them, what's *on* them and what's accessible *from* them. So why are so many people ambivalent when it comes to looking after their mobile devices and using them safely? For many, it's a case of "it's never going to happen to me", or they just take the technology and functionality as a given. But reverting to the history lesson, before 2007, a phone was, effectively, just a phone, and many of us who used them back then still haven't quite got out of that mindset.

PHYSICAL SECURITY

I'll begin by talking about physical security purely because of the nature of your mobile devices: the clue's in the name. One of the main attributes of your mobile device – in particular your smartphone – is its physical size and weight, which means that it can fit neatly into your hand, your pocket or your car's centre console so neatly. Which means that you can exploit all of that functionality and power virtually wherever you go. I know that I, for one, am rarely without mine.

However, that which most of us count as a benefit also has a downside. I'm sure that the five words my wife says most are "Have you seen my phone?" That's not normally a concern, as it's either exactly where she left in around the house, or if we're out, in her handbag (again, where she put it).

Yes, the downside to your handset's compact size and

portability is that it is easy to put down somewhere and, inversely, difficult to locate, especially if "it's on silent" (to quote my wife again). It's equally easy to accidentally damage. Ever spilled a whole mug of hot coffee over your phone? I have. What about dropping it down the toilet from your back trouser pocket? Guilty again, as are around 100,000 people a year in the United Kingdom alone. More modern phones claim to be waterproof (does that also mean cappuccinoproof?), but not so tablets, of which waterproof versions are available, but by paying a massive premium. Dropping is also a major cause of damage: how many people do you know with crazed screens? Again, ruggedised handsets and cases are available, but certainly not many of my acquaintances have them, even those in the building trade. And I don't know of *any* devices that claim to be grandchild-proof.

Please always remember what a valuable companion your mobile device is, how much you depend on it in everyday life, and consider how 'lost' you might feel if it were lost or damaged. Neither having to rebuild your contact list nor losing all of your irreplaceable family photos is a happy prospect.

Quite apart from your phone or tablet being mislaid or damaged, its compact size makes it an easy target for thieves. A stolen phone has many uses: it can be used by the opportunist thief, or 'fenced' for the financial value of a secondhand phone — considerable in the case of recent model, feature-packed devices, especially when sold on to various third-world countries.

I've already alluded to protecting what's *on* and available *from* your mobile device, and this is where the real risk from theft lies. Take a moment to consider the contents on yours. I've already mentioned your contacts and personal photos: both could be of interest (in a bad way), depending on the thief's motives. Now look at some of your device's other 'basic' functions. If you're like most people, you keep all of your text messages so you can refer back to them. And your emails. How about your map or GPS app. Does it reveal where you live, or where you've been? Have you made a record of your passwords in your notepad (*definitely* not recommended!)?

Then, of course, there are all of the apps you have downloaded and used – rich in personal information. If you don't log out of your apps when you've finished using them (in common with most people, I suspect), you risk revealing the websites you've visited, purchases you've made, your payment details and content you've watched. Your social media accounts could fall under someone else's control. Gaming apps, dating apps, betting apps, travel apps ... all reveal a vast amount of personal information that could be useful to a criminal, whether it's the one who steals your phone, or the one who ends up with it.

PROTECTING YOUR MOBILE DEVICE WHEN OUT & ABOUT

In general, the vast majority of people use their mobile devices safely and securely without any problems. There isn't a phone thief waiting around every corner, nor (hopefully) a loose kerbstone that you're going to trip over and smash your phone.

But as with most things in life, it pays to not tempt fate, and be aware of some of risks you and your phone or tablet might encounter when you're out and about with it.

I was on a train into London and it was standing room only, so I occupied the standing compartment by the door (known to train experts as a 'vestibule'). In the rear-most seats of the compartment, separated by a glass partition, were a man and a woman sharing a jumbo-sized tablet, analysing a spreadsheet. Without looking too hard, I saw the name of the business they worked for (a large, well-known corporate) and spotted that they were analysing the following 12-month revenue forecast. Fortunately for them, their work was of no interest to me, but I had become a 'shoulder surfer'. They could equally have been logging into a secure website, checking their personal bank accounts or watching adult movies. My point is that using your mobile device to do all of the things I've discussed previously is so intuitive – and our trust in our fellow human so strong – that we often pay little regard to who else may be interested in what we're doing. Whether you're on that train or other public transport, checking your bank balance during the interval at the theatre or looking at anything else in a crowded place that would better be kept to yourself, make sure there's nobody behind you, use one of the privacy filter screens on the market, or move somewhere else. Keep an eye out for those ubiquitous security cameras too … better to be sure.

I'm also frequently surprised at the number of people in cafés who leave their phones or tablets (or laptops) unattended while they go to the toilet or replenish their latte. Here, the risk is two-fold: somebody checking out what they're working on or the bank balance they're looking at if they haven't locked the screen, or a thief realising it's his (or her) lucky day. Previously, I've alluded to myself *not* being paranoid, but when I leave the bike or running machine at the gym to refill my water bottle, I always take my phone with me. Not only do I not want the expense and inconvenience of having to replace it or worry about my information security ... I'd find it very hard to complete my workout without AC/DC!

Other places that you might want to think twice about leaving devices unattended are vehicles (even if locked and the device is out of view), and hotel rooms. If you're likely to want to leave your phone or tablet in a room when you're downstairs at dinner or out and about, choose a hotel with safes in the rooms. Even then you're taking a risk, but when it comes to it, you have to trust someone, don't you? Even in your workplace, however much you trust your co-workers, keep your mobile devices to yourself. New colleagues you don't know, contractors, visitors, IT service providers, tradespeople and cleaners – all have hopefully undergone some kind of vetting, but have they? The same even goes for your home if you have people in who you don't know: someone doing work or your kids' friends. I've said it before: it's not paranoia, just good practice.

There are a number of other places where you need to make sure your device is secure too. Crowded places – especially tourist traps, railway stations and airport terminals – make excellent hunting grounds for phone thieves, whether it's from your pocket or handbag. Sometimes, unfortunately, there's the additional dimension of violence involved too. Moped-assisted thefts have become commonplace in many big cities around the world.

How many people do you see on their phones or tablets on the daily train commute? Most, in my experience. Then, on the journey home after a hard day at the office or a few after-work drinks, how many of those same people do you see having dozed off, mobile device still in hand? It's best to tuck it into your inside pocket and out of view when you feel yourself nodding.

Oh yes: I'm also the guy who once left my mobile phone on the roof of my car, only to drive off completely oblivious.

USING WI-FI HOTSPOTS

In 2016, myself and some colleagues carried out a social experiment in a pub in Berkshire. We printed some cards and placed them on the tables, advertising free Wi-Fi and the necessary access code. Within 15 minutes, quite a few customers, using their mobile devices, had hooked up to the Wi-Fi and were using social media, emailing and using their secure logins to gain access to various online accounts.

How did we know what they were doing? Because the innocuous looking guy sitting at a table in the corner, working on his laptop and enjoying a pint, was snooping on the online activity of everybody who was using the hotspot. The Wi-Fi advertised on the tables was set up on his laptop. He had a record of their names and login details. He had some bank account numbers. The names of some of their children, and their home addresses. The whole exercise was filmed for a public awareness video, including the genuine horror on the faces of the victims when we revealed what information we had about them ... and how we obtained it.

Before you have me arrested for an historic crime, I should add that our hacker was a professor in cybersecurity from a local university, we had the police's backing for our experiment, and the 'victims' had been pre-warned that something was going to happen, but not what it was. To emphasise how comparatively easy Wi-Fi snooping is to perpetrate, we had an old-school pickpocket doing the rounds in the bar at the same time, successfully lifting mobile phones, purses and wallets from some of the guests. He quite rightly pointed out that our professor was a far more dangerous 'criminal', owing to the amount and nature of information he'd obtained.

This is *not* the stuff of spy movies: using Wi-Fi hotspots in pubs, cafés, hotel rooms and other places frequented by the public is a commonplace way for criminals to facilitate fraud.

This can be done in three ways:

1. If the café, bar, hotel or wherever you are offers the use of a Wi-Fi hotspot, but it isn't secured in the same way as I hope your home or workplace router is, the traffic between it and your device can be intercepted. You would hope that the proprietor or an employee of the establishment you're patronising has not intentionally set up an insecure Wi-Fi for the purposes of snooping on you but, how do you know? Even if you have to obtain an access code from the bar or reception to be able to use the Wi-Fi, this is no indication of security.

2. By setting up a fake hotspot, in the same way as our cybersecurity professor in the pub as described above.

3. By intercepting your communications, even if you're hooked up to a secure hotspot, using one of a number of commonly-available snooping tools, in the close vicinity.

At this point, I must qualify the above by saying that you need to take care with using hotspots only if you're doing something confidential. Logging into your email or social media accounts whilst using an insecure hotspot could reveal the combination of your username/email address and password, which means you're effectively giving them away. This will not only enable the snooper to access your email or impersonate you on social media, but if you use the same login details for more than one online account, he/she could easily access all the others too. In general, it's best to avoid any transactional activities like banking, payments or purchases via hotspots too, although there are caveats.

Things you *can* do innocuously in such situations are reading the news, articles or information, watching movies, streaming music, researching (but not booking) holidays and a multitude of other activities for which you don't need a secure login. So, if you have to enter a username and password to download information or images from a media site, using a hotspot probably isn't the best way to do it. Wait until you get home or to the office (again, as long as the router is secured), use your mobile data allowance or get a mobile broadband 'dongle'.

I've read many recommendations that you should use a secure VPN (virtual private network) for activities like email or accessing the company network. This is fine as long as the VPN is administered by your organisation and you have a secure login to it. However, there are a massive number of VPN products on the market, and you need to be very careful which one you choose, as VPN providers are in the privileged position of being able to monitor all of the information that's sent via their service.

APPS ON YOUR MOBILE DEVICE

Part of the reason for the mobile revolution and the demand for the latest technology is the extraordinary number and range of apps available for devices. The inverse is also true, with such avid app development being largely driven by users' demand to both make life more convenient and, in some cases, impress their acquaintances with their range of online toys.

Apps have certainly changed most people's lives. Recent generations of mobile websites have certainly made things easier than entering a website address and trying to read a standard-format website on a small screen. And in some cases, of course, they do a fine job, especially when an app just isn't the appropriate interface. But many would say that there's no substitute for apps, with their instant access, intuitive operation and easy navigation – whether you're banking, gaming, getting your entertainment, buying a car, dating or just reading the news.

As I've mentioned previously, however, the more universally something is adopted, the greater target it will be for malicious or less honest factions to exploit it. Not only that, but as a rule of thumb, the easier to use and more accessible technology becomes, the more vulnerable it becomes.

That's why I'd like to offer you some advice on the safe use of mobile apps.

Downloading mobile apps

The key item of advice here is to search and install apps only from the authorised source for your smartphone or tablet's operating system. For your iPhone, that's the App Store, for your Android device it's Google Play, and for Microsoft Windows devices (including Windows-powered Nokia devices), it's the Microsoft Store.

The reason for this is that there are many 'rogue' apps out there, which the developers have either tried to get listed on the authorised sources listed above but failed for one reason or another, have previously been listed but their app has been removed, or which haven't been applied for at all because they know they'll fall foul of the rules. The main reasons that these apps *aren't* listed are:

- They may contain malware, which could enable cybercriminals to take control of your handset, make calls, incur charges via premium text messages without your permission, become part of a botnet for disruptive purposes, lock access until a ransom is paid or send and intercept SMS and voicemail messages.
- They may promote illegal, irresponsible or dangerous behaviour.
- They may incite extremism and/or terrorism.
- They may contain offensive, obscene or otherwise illegal content, or material inappropriate to the app's age rating.
- They may be of a quality inferior to that acceptable by the store.
- They may infringe copyright, either containing copyright-protected content or being blatantly pirated versions of authentic apps (sometimes known as 'cracked' apps).
- They may violate the stores' rules for how apps can be developed, or how they function.

The fact that I've advised you to download apps only from authorised sources implies that they are available elsewhere, and this is indeed the case. Anyone can carry out a simple online search to locate spurious app stores, of which there are many. Unauthorised apps are also freely available on bulletin boards and peer-to-peer networks. I'm sure that many of the apps available from these non-Apple, Android or Windows stores don't fall into any of the categories listed above. But, as in many online scenarios, is it worth the risk? To the normal user, *I don't think so*. Installing unauthorised apps normally also means modifying the firmware on your device so that it can run them (you may have heard the expression 'jailbreaking' when talking about Apple devices, or 'rooting', applied to Android devices). This is done frequently, it's perfectly legal and you can easily find someone to do it for you or even follow one of the many videos on YouTube. However, I definitely don't recommend that you do it as (a) invalidates your guarantee, (b) it contravenes your end-user licence agreement, and (c) it leaves your device wide open to malware infection.

Do some due diligence before downloading your apps. Read the description thoroughly to make sure it does what you want it to do. Read third-party, unbiased reviews. Talk to friends or colleagues. Double-check the purchase cost, but also to see if there are any ongoing costs, and the necessity for in-app purchases to unlock the functions you need (this may apply whether the initial download is free or paid-for). Check the information provided under the description, including whether it is compatible with your device, and the size, to ensure there's sufficient memory on your device.

App permissions

You've downloaded your app and are trying out the features. You need to be aware that many apps interact with other apps or data on your mobile device in order to provide you with these features, or simply to work at all. At the risk of stating the obvious, a photo manipulation app, for example, will require access to your saved photos and possibly your camera (so will social media apps if you want to share your pics). A navigation app will need access to your current and intended location in order to provide you with accurate directions and anticipated time of arrival.

It is generally agreed in app development circles that developers should request only data and features directly necessary for the app to operate, which explains why your app will probably pop up a message to ask you to authorise (or reject) permissions such as these, but some may not. Some apps, however, may request *additional* permissions over and above those strictly necessary for the particular app being accessed, to function.

You may even find that some apps will not alert you to the permissions they need to access other apps or data. The key here, is to read the small print. When you've found the app in your store that you want to download, before you do so, scroll down to the developer's privacy policy. This contains a lot more than standard terms and conditions, in fact I'd say it's an essential read, however arduous it might seem. One of the main (and somewhat contentious) terms is that the developer may share your data with third parties or their parent company. The privacy policy should specify what permissions the app will need in order to function and provide added features, and rather than you having to click 'accept', the act of downloading represents your acceptance.

If you're not comfortable with the permissions requested, search for an alternative app in your authorised store, or if you've already downloaded the app and you get a pop-up requesting approval for an in-app payment, you can always deny permission.

App costs are not necessarily all up front

Whether you have paid to download an app or not, it could end up costing you money anyway, in two ways.

If you use apps whilst your mobile device is connected to the internet via 4G or 3G – in other words using your data allowance – it will use some of that allowance and, in theory, end up costing you if you reach your data limit for the month (or whatever plan you have with your network). However, even if you don't consciously use your apps when out and about, they could still be consuming data whilst they're refreshing in the background. If you're abroad, depending on your whereabouts, this could incur roaming charges if you haven't turned off your device's data. You can generally control via your settings whether you want your apps to refresh in the background or not. Most networks offer apps or other tools to help you check your real-time usage quickly and easily.

What you probably need to be more conscious of, however, are apps that offer in-app purchases (sometimes abbreviated to IAPs, thanks to the tech world's never-ending demand for acronyms). Many apps offer optional extras, which are, effectively, 'unlocked' in return for payment. Generally, this applies to free-to-download and inexpensive apps, rather than the costlier apps where the features tend to (but don't always) come as standard.

The most common examples of apps with in-app purchases are games, where you often have to pay to move up to a higher level, speed up gameplay or acquire virtual payment tokens or 'properties' (assets used within the game). There are also now quite a few apps designed to increase efficiency for businesses, which feature in-app purchases to gain more functionality.

When you've found the app that you want in your app store, scroll down the description to see if it requires in-app purchases. If it does, click on it to drill down into what those purchases are, how much they cost and if you consider them worthwhile. If you're not paying for the app in the first place, it's not so important to do this as you're not risking anything, but if it's a paid-for app and you download it, you've made the commitment, so you might feel obliged to take advantage of the additional features.

If you're using the app and do decide to make an in-app purchase, you will be prompted to accept the terms & conditions by entering your app store login details, or optionally identifying yourself with your fingerprint (in the case of devices with that feature).

As an adult with the freedom to control your own device usage and finances, the only issue you may face is your in-app purchases getting out of control and exceeding comfortable levels. Many online gambling sites offer a wide choice of ways to pay, including making deposits on casino sites which are added to your phone bill. Personally, I'm not a fan of gambling, but I do think this payment method makes it too easy, as it's a kind of credit account.

If your children (or other young people in your care) are using your device – and have access to games, entertainment content or other apps which offer in-app purchases – this can be problematic if you're not aware of their activity. In theory, this can happen only when the young person concerned has access to your login details and/or their own fingerprint recognition on their or your smartphone or tablet. Personally, I know of lots of children who do, indeed have this capability, in many cases because their parents just want a quiet life. Generally, payments for in-app purchases are added to the bill of the device user, and it's not uncommon for parents to get quite a shock when their children have been left to their own devices.

Some mobile handsets give you the facility to disable in-app purchases altogether. It's easy to set these restrictions in your settings, but you can also find plenty of instructions and advice via an online search.

DISPOSAL

Exercise the same care when disposing of your mobile device that you should have during its working life with you – whether you're selling, gifting, donating, part-exchanging or scrapping it. As emphasised above, your smartphone or tablet potentially contains – and provides access to – a vast amount of information, some of it confidential or sensitive, which you don't want to fall into the wrong hands for a variety of reasons. Apps, emails and email accounts, bookmarks, browsing history, notes, photos, music ... in fact everything that you've added to the device since you acquired it, should be *properly* deleted and the device re-set before you dispose of it.

For your Android phone, enable encryption before applying the factory reset. If it's an Apple iPhone, it already has hardware encryption by default, a feature that as a user, you can't disable. I recommend that you download and use a reputable data deletion tool to be confident that your device is 'clean'.

Before you re-set your device, ensure that it has been backed up, either to your cloud backup as described in 'Backing up your mobile devices', previously, or by syncing it to your computer. Check that the backup has been successful before deleting all that data.

And here's the environmental bit: if you are scrapping your device, once you're satisfied that the data is thoroughly deleted, take it to a proper licensed disposal facility which will ensure that it is dismantled, and the components recycled responsibly. Alternatively, your device may still be in good working order and of use to someone in your country or around the world who couldn't otherwise afford to own one. There are many charities who organise this, but I repeat, always delete!

1.3

DOWNLOADING AND FILE SHARING

Downloading and file sharing are both very popular ways to obtain entertainment, images, software applications and other digital items.

Because today's world seems to have become digitally-driven – at home, at work and at play – and bandwidth and download speeds have steadily increased over time, downloading has become by far the most popular way to obtain any digital 'assets' (as well as streaming, of course). I can't remember the last time I bought an album on CD or a film on DVD, and all of my existing disks have been consigned to the attic. For years, I haven't ordered anything smaller than the occasional specialist large format or canvas print. Nor have I been into my local computer store or stationery retailer to buy software – whether it's word processing, antivirus or a newer version of my computer's operating system. Instead, I download *everything*: it's more convenient, I can get and use it instantly, and it's frequently cheaper. Even massive graphics files can be moved around between users by using one of the many cloud-based high-speed transfer services available today.

File sharing is different from downloading. Sometimes known as 'file swapping', it can be described as the practice of accessing or sharing files by one or more users – either privately or publicly. There are many file-sharing sites on the internet and the most common types of files uploaded by their users for others to share are videos, photos, computer software, games and all kinds of documents.

The type of file sharing I am focusing on here is via peer-to-peer (P2P) networks, where shared files on other users' computers are indexed on directory servers. Peer-to-peer file sharing can be particularly attractive for some users, as what's downloaded – be it films, music, images, documents or software – is free. Ever since the dawn of peer-to-peer networks many years ago, many gained a bad reputation – one that continues today, and with good reason (well, several reasons, actually). More below.

File syncing and sharing services such as Dropbox and Google Drive are also types of file sharing. Services such as there are generally reputable and a widely-used method of sharing and distributing information, particularly in the commercial context but also increasingly for private individuals. Such services feature varying levels of access privilege, meaning that you can specify who you choose to securely share your data, to the exclusion of others. Getting these access privileges right is absolutely essential if you wish to maintain security, as is observing good practice when it comes to devising and protecting passwords.

DOWNLOADING

The overarching advice applying to downloading is that you should always do so from an authorised source for that product.

So what *are* authorised sources? Manufacturers

and their authorised distributors of films, games and software. Within 'distributors' I'm including television and telecommunications providers as well as legitimate online retailers: for software products, legitimate on-line retailers and app stores as well as manufacturers: for music downloads, legitimate online retailers and download services, as well as publishers.

I strongly recommend that you don't buy/download from anywhere else, for a number of reasons.

1. The product you are downloading could be infected with any number of types of malware, which are described elsewhere in this book. If this happens, you'll wish you'd gone straight to the legitimate source and paid the money. A legitimate website is also more likely to have robust security in place.
2. You could be put at risk by not just the files. Using the website itself could expose you to fraud by either spreading malware or fraudulently capturing your details – which could be used for financial or identity fraud (or both), and/or be sold on within criminal networks.
3. The site may be contravening copyright law, if the product you're downloading is a pirated version (this is very prevalent with films, games and software). Not only might the quality be sub-standard (and in some cases the product unusable), but in the case of games, you won't be entitled to updates or the developer's user support. Depending on where you live in the world, you may be breaking the law and risking harsh penalties. On top of that, you should spare a thought for the companies who make and distribute the authentic products. Not only are they losing revenue, but their employees

– ordinary men and women making an honest living – are also at risk of losing their jobs because sales are suffering as a result of pirating. Similar to when you buy a designer T-shirt or handbag at the local market. Check that the site has the copyright holder's permission to sell and distribute the product.

There are many websites offering 'free and legal' downloads of anything from films and music to software, as well as those offering mobile apps. Without knowing more about individual examples, I can't tell you whether they're legitimate and safe, or illegal and unsafe. It's 'buyer beware': you need to do your research, check reviews, talk to other people and use your intuition to figure out whether to download from these sites or not.

Unfortunately, as with everything in life, nothing's fool-proof. Free versions of software from the genuine vendor are generally safe … it's just that they tend to be 'lite' on features and in the case of antivirus products, don't get updated as frequently as the paid-for versions. However, in September 2017, *CCleaner,* a reputable and ubiquitous tool used globally to clean and optimise Windows computers, was discovered to contain malicious code which it added to the operating system on which it was installed (Version 5.33, incidentally). This certainly wasn't a deliberate deed by the manufacturer, but an act perpetrated by hackers who had inserted a 'backdoor' into the software, enabling remote access to infected machines. Just three months before, *CCleaner's* manufacturer had been acquired by one of the most reputable antivirus vendors in the business, embarrassingly for all concerned (except the hackers!)

FILE SHARING

P2P (peer-to-peer) networks are systems that let you make certain files available to anyone, anywhere who has the same file-sharing software. It is this degree of anonymity and non-regulation that causes problems. The fact that files are moved around the world by complete strangers makes legitimate users particularly vulnerable to issues.

The greatest threat is malware. Once a user has either deliberately or inadvertently uploaded an infected file, the malware spreads out of control from computer to computer (peer-to-peer), putting all users who download the file at risk of fraud and identity theft. Certain strains of malware – known as remote access trojans (with the appropriate acronym of RATs) can even be used to activate your webcam and record your every move when in front of your computer. Malware can be disguised in many types of files – both legitimate and pirated.

As alluded to previously, it is not just the files that pose a threat, but the peer-to-peer file sharing site itself. Apart from infecting it with malware, it could capture your IP address for others to see and potentially misuse.

Also, it is commonplace for peer-to-peer file sharing networks to require you to disable your computer's firewall in order to share the files. Given the nature of these networks that I have described above, doing this is asking for trouble, as even the briefest closure could leave you wide open to attacks. Criminals using the site could gain illicit access to your computer for any number of sinister reasons, whilst others could seize the opportunity to exploit any vulnerabilities in the sharing software itself. In participating – albeit inadvertently – in the spread of malware, you could easily, in turn, be infecting other users.

Another potential issue is that you could be exposed to illegal or inappropriate content, disguised as legitimate, harmless files. Pornographic, violent and extremist content are often hidden behind the mask of respectable files on peer-to-peer file sharing services.

And again, there's the problem of breaking the law by downloading films, TV programmes, music tracks, software, games and photos that are protected by copyright. Doing this inadvertently is no protection from law enforcement.

THINGS YOU MAY DO ONLINE & WHY YOU NEED TO BE CAREFUL

Sometimes it seems that everything we can do offline, we can now do online too. That's not true, of course, but it certainly applies to buying and paying for products and services, from your weekly shopping to a fishing licence.

The internet has brought us massive benefits when it comes to convenience, choice, time and often, price. In 30 minutes or less, we can play games against thousands of adversaries around the world, place a bet on the 3.45 and research and pay for our summer holiday, from our smartphone and without moving from our chair. I swear that in a few generations' time, our descendants will be born with less functional legs and one arm bent and hand grasped as if using a mobile phone.

You'd need a whole bookshelf if I advised you on keeping safe with everything you pay money for online, so I've mentioned online gaming, gambling and travel booking, as a representative sample.

QR CODES

If you mention the term 'QR code' to people, some will know what you're talking about and others will look at you blankly. Until, that is, you show them an example of this two-dimensional, 'matrix' type of barcode, when most people will instantly recognise it. Many do still not, however, know its function.

Another brief history lesson: the system was invented back in 1994 by a Japanese company to track vehicles and components during the manufacturing process. Many other commercial applications followed, including security passes, cashless vending, transport ticketing, libraries, inventory and biochemical research, to name but a handful. However, it didn't take long for QR (short for 'quick response') codes to be adopted by marketeers to provide consumers with an easy way to access the information they wanted them to see, usually the home page, a specific product page or a campaign landing page on their website. Marketing QR codes can also be used to send text messages and emails, initiate phone calls, connect to Wi-Fi networks, download coupons and initiate purchases.

You'll find marketing QR codes in a variety of places, but most commonly in newspapers and magazines, on posters and store displays, and perhaps on product packaging to either guide you to user instructions or cross-sell the rest of the manufacturer's range.

QR codes are not human-readable. Instead, you need a QR code reader / scanner app on your mobile device which interacts with its camera. There are many available from your app store, featuring varying degrees of sophistication, some handsets and tablets are supplied with reader apps out of the box, and some mobile web browsers incorporate them. All you have to do is open the app, aim your device's camera at the QR code, and the software in the app does the rest, including automatically opening the destination web page, initiating the phone call or message, downloading the coupon and so on.

The fact that you can't read QR codes by eye also brings a considerable potential downside: you can't be sure exactly what the act of scanning them will instruct your mobile device to do. And neither myself nor anybody else can advise you on which ones are legitimate, and which ones aren't, because I can't read them either.

Earlier in the book, I talked about malware-laden websites which, when visited, lead to your devices being infected. How will you know if the QR code you're scanning leads to one of these websites? Equally, a fake code could access your camera, contacts or navigation data, send premium rate texts or commandeer your device as part of a botnet.

Since anybody can create the codes using simple tools, it isn't difficult for somebody with the requisite knowledge to insert malware into it and replace or modify an original, legitimate tag. Admittedly, this is more likely to have happened to a poster pasted on to a derelict shop window advertising a local grunge gig than in your local newspaper or a glossy magazine. But unfortunately, my work has made me quite cynical, and any of the above can and do happen.

Some QR code reader / scanner apps claim to offer additional security by vetting the code and warning you if it's malicious. I can't recommend these (or otherwise), and instead, remember that – as in all things online – discretion is the better part of valour.

1.4

GAMING, GAMBLING, TRAVELLING AND TICKETS

ONLINE GAMING

Online gaming has captured the hearts and minds (and in a lot of cases, many waking hours) of millions of people around the world. It can be relaxing, exciting, even educational. But it can also be expensive, addictive and even potentially, dangerous ... in a number of ways.

Here, I need to use some technical jargon: the games played online with other participants are known as Massive Multiplayer Online Role Playing Games (MMORPGs or MMOs), which means that your fellow players (or adversaries, however you think of them), make up a large online community of anonymous strangers, frequently using aliases instead of real names. It may be, of course, that you prefer to play against just one or a few friends.

Most multiplayer games also offer communication between players – either with an integrated chat feature (typing in messages in the same way as instant messaging platforms) or verbally, using a headset. These discussions, threads and conversations are unfiltered and unmoderated.

It's tricky to put the risks in order as these games have so many features which can cause problems, so please don't regard any of the following comments as more important or relevant than others.

Hidden costs in online gaming

Of course, we all have to accept that whether you're obtaining a game to play on your computer, games console or mobile device, there may be an upfront cost in purchasing the game in the first place. Some developers enable you to download the game installer but make it clear that there is a cost for the 'full' version, others are clearer in that to play the game at all, you need to pay up front to download it. Both of these approaches seem perfectly reasonable to me. Playing many games also requires additional expenditure after you've purchased and downloaded – for example, to unlock features, play at higher skill levels or purchase in-game properties. The more mainstream, reputable developers make this clear before you download the game, and you should be happy in your own mind that you're willing to spend money to enjoy the game's full experience.

Unfortunately, many people tend to get carried away and the expenditure gets out of control. When it's one your children playing the game on your device, this is something you need a keep a keen eye on. It's not uncommon for parents to receive shockingly-high payment card statements or mobile phone bills (depending on the game's charging model) as a result of their children's online gaming activities.

Potential for abuse

If some of the other people you may be playing online games against are friends and/or family members, hopefully you can assume your communications via the chat or speech facilities will be safe. As mentioned above, however, it's quite possible that you could be playing against total strangers, whose real names and locations are unknown to you.

Let me emphasise that most online gamers merely want to enjoy the game they've chosen to play online and interact civilly and constructively with the other players they've 'met'. However, some are extremely competitive – even to the point of fanaticism and, unfortunately, frustration and anger can spill over into abuse targeted at other players. Others – who may or not be serious gamers – simply use gaming as an excuse to spread abuse, or target individuals purely to make their gaming experience less enjoyable. This is often referred to as 'griefing'. Online gaming can also be exploiting by bullies – either exclusively, in addition to other online channels or in addition to physical bullying.

Reputable online games platforms give you the option to block and report such gamers. I strongly advise you to do so, and don't rise to the bait by responding.

There are other, more sinister types of abuse you could be exposed to on multi-player games where you don't know other players, which I shall loosely term as grooming.

Grooming is frequently directed at children, but not exclusively so. When gaming (as you would on social media or in chatrooms), you need to be aware if you're being approached by either stalkers or dating fraudsters. By the former, I mean someone either known or not known to you who is taking an unhealthy and often overbearing interest in you. By the latter, I mean someone, for example, posing as a member of the armed forces serving abroad who takes an interest in you, but ultimately only to defraud you out of your savings. These 'men' and 'women' are generally organised criminal gangs, commonly working out of West Africa or Eastern Europe. They will use whatever communication channel is effective to ply their trade. If you do get approached or, even worse, fall victim to such illicit activity, you should report it to both law enforcement and the gaming platform.

The other type of grooming I'd like to mention is to do with extremism. Terrorist groups around the world – and their members or sympathisers in your own country – have become experts as using the internet for recruiting and fundraising purposes. Again, multi-player gaming platforms are awash with impressionable, idealistic people. Once again, any approaches you or your children experience should be reported to the appropriate anti-terror authority in your country.

Other issues

It's commonly agreed that one of the main issues associated with online gaming is the potential desire to spend many hours beating your adversaries or achieving the next level. What starts out as harmless fun can encroach on – and even start to take over – your life. In extreme cases, the long hours spent online, often without a proper break, can result in addiction, which has frequently been compared with addiction to alcohol or drugs. Left to continue, this can lead to tiredness, poor performance at work and relationship breakdowns. Fanatical gamers have been known to ignore their personal hygiene because they "don't have time" to wash or change their clothes. Recorded extreme cases include the suicide of a 13 year old Chinese boy in 2004, after he jumped off of a 24-story building in re-enactment of a scene from a game, a 28-year-old South Korean man who died of heart failure after playing a game for 50 hours non-stop in a gaming café, and an addicted gamer – again in China – who murdered another gamer who borrowed and then sold a virtual object within an online role-playing game. As I've said, these are extreme ... and rare.

I believe that some developers employ psychologists to create game play aspects to keep their games addictive, and gamers continuing to pay their monthly subscription fees. Many health authorities are advising people to self-impose a limit on their gaming in order to avoid the type of problems associated with over-indulgence. Indeed, in China, online gaming is regarded as such a social issue that the government has clamped down on addictive games and attempted to limit the time that under 18 year olds spend playing them. How effective these measures have been isn't certain.

Then, there's the issue of revealing too much information.

One of the main ways by which security experts advise you to protect your finances and identity is by keeping your confidential information close to your chest. This ranges from not revealing your date of birth on profiles or using names of family members, pets or football teams in passwords, to not providing unnecessary personal information in response to emails. Bear this in mind when setting up your user profile – for example, if you have to state your date of birth or mother's maiden name, make it someone else's, or just make them up. If you're using the messaging or chat features to communicate with other, unknown gamers, keep the conversation about the game, and not your phone number or which school your children attend. In addition, when you're disposing of your unwanted computer, mobile device or console – whether gifting or donating it, selling it or scrapping it – be very sure to *thoroughly delete* all the information held on it such as personal data and account details, to avoid it falling into the wrong hands.

Elsewhere in this book we have discussed malware, and the various devious methods used by criminals to spread it. The potential for the device via which you're gaming to be infected by malware is very real, in several different ways:

If the game you're playing is hosted on a website for which you've received a link, for example in an email, social media post or text message, research the site first, then manually type in the address you know to be authentic. It's simple for a cybercriminal to set up a fraudulent site using an address that's almost indiscernible from the real thing, but that will in reality be infected with malware or designed to capture confidential information such as payment details. The site should also be secure, which you can check if the address begins with 'https' and there's a locked padlock in the address bar.

Malware can also be picked up by downloading cheats and/or pirated games. Just don't even consider downloading counterfeit games or, for that matter, any other software. You could face harsh penalties for contravening copyright laws, but also put at the risk the livelihood of people earning an honest living designing, developing and distributing the real thing.

Online gaming and young people

I've already mentioned racking up costs as a potential hazard associated with young people's gaming, but there are others too.

Games are generally rated by age group, as well as having warnings about the type of content, if applicable (such as if they feature light, moderate or heavy sex, violence or bad language). Some developers are more diligent than others about how prominent and clear these warnings are, so it is important for you – as a parent, guardian or other responsible adult – to check this information before buying games for your children, or generally keep an eye on what they're playing. Naturally, parents have differing ideas about what is appropriate for their child's age, so you may consider content that your child may be legitimately exposed to in the context of the game's rating, to be *inappropriate* for them. Check reviews and speak to other parents and – if you can – play (or experience) the game yourself to check it out.

Many gamers are minors, and despite the existence of minimum age ratings, it's easy for most children to access games, either in the privacy of their room, out and about on their mobile device or maybe at friends' houses. Unfortunately, because of anonymity of other players, the messaging and chat platforms can be exploited by others for the grooming and – ultimately – sexual exploitation of your child. As is the case on social media platforms, this generally takes the form of an adult posing as a child, developing a friendly relationship and then convincing the child to take some kind of action, which could be sharing images or a physical meeting.

As with all online activities, it is essential to work with your child to explain in an age-appropriate way how to protect themselves, as well as taking an interest in their activities and keeping abreast of the latest developments. There are also many types of technological approaches, the most commonplace being monitoring and control software and ISP-level filters, though these would not detect who your child is talking to, or what they're saying, on gaming or social media platforms. Encourage your child to talk to you – or another trusted adult – about any such approaches. If it happens, report it to the police and the gaming platform.

It has been proved that there is a definite link between gaming and gambling, most prevalently in children and young people. Some games include gambling – even virtual roulette wheels and fruit machines – within the content, so the interest in gambling could be planted. Some go so far as to charge real money for gambling chips or spins. So it's no wonder that the boundaries between 'innocent' gambling in games, and actual online gambling, become less discernible (this also being the case with many adults).

I've already mentioned the importance of moderating how much time you spend online gaming. In the context of children and young people, there have been many statistics quoted over the years about how many hours are consumed – and potentially misspent – on online gaming. Many parents simply say: "too many". Youngsters commonly spend many hours in their rooms playing online games. Many adults (and some children) will agree that this can lead to a number of issues, including the inability to develop interpersonal skills, poor academic progress, eyesight problems, posture problems, insomnia, tiredness and obesity. There's also a higher chance that they'll be exposed the problems I've outlined above. As a parent, you probably know what is and isn't healthy, but it's certainly worth reading research and talking to other parents.

ONLINE GAMBLING

There have always been casinos, poker, bingo, sports betting, and lotteries. There have always been serious gamblers, professional gamblers and those who enjoy the occasional 'flutter'.

Enter online gambling, which has been around since the mid-1990s and has seen a spectacular increase in popularity, with many thousands of operators. Casual and serious gamblers alike can participate in all forms of betting mentioned above, from the comfort of their living room, or the convenience of their smartphone. They can even place a bet on their country's next leader or the chance of a particular kind of weather on a particular date in the future.

Any kind of gambling has both fans and detractors. Whatever your stance, the following are online gambling 'certainties':

- You have a massive choice of companies to use and things to gamble on
- You can gamble at any time, from any location where you can go online
- The chances of being defrauded are as real as with anything else you do online that involves payments
- You don't always know who you're dealing with
- It is as easy to get carried away with how much money you're gambling online (as is also the case in a bookmaker's shop or at the races) – some would say it's even easier.
- It's easy to get carried away with how much time you're spending gambling online (normally closely associated with my previous point)

A quick internet search will reveal some of the issues associated with online gambling. Addiction, fraud and money-laundering appear with alarming frequency.

Of course, it's perfectly feasible to gamble online without encountering any of these problems – and millions of people do – but it's my job to make you aware of how to do it safely, and what can go wrong.

Problem gambling

In many countries, advertising and sponsorship by tobacco companies is banned. I frequently ask myself why – in many of those countries – the same doesn't go for gambling websites and bookmakers. I say "in many of those countries" because many do ban gambling advertising, and in fact in others, online gambling itself is banned, or restricted to one degree or another. Like nicotine, gambling can become highly addictive. In my opinion, that's more likely when done online, behind closed doors. The advertising makes it look so attractive, with the promise of free starter bets and large bonuses.

In the previous section of this book about online gaming, I mentioned some of the potential consequences of gaming addiction: ranging from tiredness and poor performance at work to, tragically, suicide. Like gaming, unfettered gambling can 'take over' your life, but with the additional potential consequences brought about by losing large sums of money. This is why it's desperately important to set affordable limits and adhere to them, however tempting it may be to carry on.

Accounts of heavy borrowing including payday loans to fuel gambling habits and cover debts are commonplace. Theft – possibly couched as 'borrowing without asking' from friends or relatives – isn't uncommon. Gambling anything from the weekly pay packet to the family fortune isn't uncommon either, leading to the misery of debt and family breakdown. Also, you may have seen cases of people prosecuted for stealing from their employer to fund their addiction. Clearly, the "just one more bet" mindset when you're already in the red rarely has a positive outcome.

There are many help organisations funded by the

industry either as part of their corporate social responsibility programmes, or because they are required to do so as part of their regulation. They can provide help for problem gamblers and, importantly, potential problem gamblers. If you fall into either of these categories, I urge you to contact them.

The risk of fraud

There are several ways that you can become a victim of financial fraud, identity theft or both, through online gambling.

In countries where online casinos and other forms of internet gambling are permitted, there is generally relatively poor regulation. This makes it difficult to know who actually operates the business and whether the stated odds of winning (and the rewards themselves) are accurate. It also makes it hard to pursue legal action if you find that you've been cheated out of either your stake or your winnings. Remember that you cannot determine an operator's county of origin from the website address suffix, as anybody, anywhere can register any suffix.

Another risk to online gamblers is fake or copycat websites. These can take the form of a site which has been set up from scratch by fraudsters, which, to a gambler looking for a fresh experience, will appear as just another one of the thousands on offer. Such sites can defraud you in one (or both) of two ways: either by capturing confidential personal and payment details that you provide when opening an account, or by infecting your computer or mobile device with the type of malware used to capture your financial transactions, and other information on your device. Alternatively, they can be set up to mimic well-known, reputable sites – looking and working like the real thing. In this case, there are very few clues that you are actually paying out to cybercriminals.

Always be wary that such sites (and, increasingly, rogue mobile apps) exist. Addresses of fake sites are often almost indiscernible from those of authentic ones, with perhaps a different letter or punctuation to deceive you. Don't click on links to gambling sites in emails, text messages or on social media, but determine the correct address of reputable sites and type it in yourself. If using anything other than a reputable, mainstream site, check online reviews and forums to determine whether they are genuine, and the quality of the betting experience.

This one may seem obvious, but you should never share too much information. This applies to when you set up your account and when you communicate with other people – face-to-face, by email or in social media. When setting up your account for example, if you're asked for your mother's maiden name as a means of authentication, give another surname that you will be able to remember easily. And, of course, revealing banking passwords is strictly off-limits. Some sites – in particular bingo sites – offer a chat facility. Enjoy the banter but do be guarded about the information you reveal to others.

My final point doesn't fall under the heading of fraud but be aware that some credit card companies categorise betting as 'cash' and may levy a fixed charge from the date of payment, or the equivalent interest to as if you had taken a cash withdrawal.

Gambling and young people

In the section on gaming, I talked about the fact that games are age-rated and also the undoubted link between gaming and gambling.

Most countries quite rightly impose a minimum legal age for gambling. Reputable gambling sites observe this … it wouldn't be worth the reputational damage or penalties suffered if they did not. However, online, it is simple to claim to be older than you actually are (as is the case with alcohol and tobacco-related sites). It has been known for children in their early teens to develop gambling problems.

If you have or are otherwise responsible for children below the legal gambling age, talk to them about the dangers, especially if they are already keen gamers. Without becoming oppressive, work with them to encourage healthy online habits, and also consider parental software to keep an eye on their activity in the background.

HOLIDAY & TRAVEL BOOKING

The vast majority of holidays and travel is researched and booked online nowadays, be it a train journey to a business meeting, a short break, a family holiday or a religious pilgrimage. The world is at your fingertips.

With leisure travel in particular, there's an additional, emotional dimension: the anticipation of spending a short break with a loved one, or the excitement of your children when you book the annual summer holiday – whether it's a caravan by the sea or an all-inclusive luxury resort. Which means that if anything should go wrong, it's considerably more than your money that's at stake.

Unfortunately, fraud relating to holidays and travel has become commonplace, and the trend is increasing. Internet users looking for holiday accommodation are a group that's targeted very frequently. Properties such as villas, apartments, park homes and ski lodges are fraudulently advertised on legitimate accommodation listing websites as well as buying/selling sites and via social media. By 'fraudulently', I mean that the accommodation or flight has been advertised either by a scammer who has no connection with it, or it's completely non-existent. Victims have been known to turn up either at the airport – or at the accommodation itself – only to be left stranded, with no possibility of getting their money back because they've paid by bank transfer. It is generally the responsibility of the prospective holidaymaker to contact the advertiser direct, and herein lies the problem.

Typically, you'll see an advertisement, or otherwise find the accommodation in an internet search. You'll communicate with the advertiser, agree that it's what you want and when you want it, and in common with most holidays, pay in advance. The normal sequence of events is that the advertiser will request payment directly into his or her bank account, giving the reason that they don't accept payment cards – which would be perfectly reasonable for a private owner – or it is so close to the date of the let that they require the money instantly to secure the accommodation. Many transactions carried out in this way are perfectly legitimate, but you should be wary, because this is also the favoured modus operandi of holiday fraudsters. When you fail to be able to contact the advertiser by any means after the money has been transferred, you'll realise that you've been defrauded. Worse still, many victims actually turn up to the accommodation, only to find it doesn't exist, or it *does* exist but has been rented out by the legitimate owner. Their travel may have involved a flight, and the chances are that they won't be able to find alternative accommodation at such short notice. By the time you report the fraud to the police and your bank, the fraudster will be uncontactable, and your money will be untraceable. Depending on where you live, your bank may refuse to reimburse the payment on the grounds that you haven't carried out due diligence on the advertiser.

It's essential, first of all, to make sure the accommodation actually exists by researching it thoroughly online, checking it out on other accommodation sites (many legitimate owners advertise in several places), on Google Maps and on review sites such as TripAdvisor. Call the owner or legitimate agent personally on a number you have found independently. And never pay by bank transfer, however desperate you are to secure the property.

The process described above can also apply to flights and package holidays. More often, these involve fake websites which are set up with a spurious identity, or to emulate the sites of reputable travel booking businesses. They may even accept payment by card, but it will be to a fraudster's account, not that of a legitimate business. Or they may tell you that their card payment facility isn't working. I know of people who have lost very large sums of money paid for pilgrimages to Mecca for their entire extended families … involving both flights and accommodation. Not only have they lost their savings, they also feel they have failed to commit to a requirement of their faith.

Fraudulent sites can also lead to you being defrauded by capturing confidential personal and payment details that you provide when booking, or by infecting your computer or mobile device with some kind of malware. Again, read reviews and make sure the company is an accredited member of a reputable travel trade association.

Another type of holiday fraud which has been around for a long time involves fake competitions. You receive a text, email or message via social media informing you that you've won a holiday, but there's some kind of up-front payment required, normally described as an administration fee. If you fancy the holiday and pay the fee, unfortunately, it's the last you'll see of your money.

The best advice to avoid such scams is to thoroughly research holidays and travel before you book. Do this by looking for reviews, talking in person to the advertiser on the phone, checking the location on Google Maps and doing a reverse image search to make sure the image hasn't been 'lifted' from an authentic site. Never pay by bank transfer (however desperate you are to secure the holiday or however good the price), always pay by credit card if you can, as this method does provide additional protection. Always better to be safe than sorry.

If booking a holiday via a website, check that there's some kind of protection, such as membership of a recognised travel trade body (this isn't always the case though, especially in the case of 'noticeboard' listing sites). Always type in the address of the website you want to visit rather than following a link in an email, social media post or text, as fraudsters often create fake websites with almost indiscernible spelling changes. These websites can take your payment, which will and before paying, make sure the payment page is secure by checking that the address begins with 'https://' ('s' is short for 'secure') and that there's a locked padlock in the address panel.

Finally, in this section, I'm going to offer you some advice that's related to holidays and travel, but not fraud. It's not anything to do with booking … it just seems like the most appropriate place to mention it. When you're away enjoying yourself, it's highly tempting to post photos on social media. That's your choice, but consider that social media is the modern burglar's best friend. If you've left your home unoccupied while you're away, that's tantamount to inviting burglars round to help themselves. It happened to a former England footballer, who posted snaps of his skiing holiday only to be burgled by a gang who carried out a series of raids on similar, luxury properties. I understand that many insurance companies now refuse to pay out on claims for burglaries committed in this way on grounds of negligence, so please be aware of this.

BUYING TICKETS

There are many similarities between booking holidays or travel and buying events tickets online.

There's something compelling about seeing your favourite band or the team you support live, with nothing quite like being there, on the day. Unable to buy tickets from the official sources because of demand – or you've left it too late – you look on an auction site or spot an ad on social media. Many of these ads are quite genuine, but they also provide scammers with an ideal opportunity to defraud you by telling you to pay by bank transfer for tickets which don't turn up when expected, or fakes ... which you'll only discover when you're refused entry on the day. I spoke to a supporter of an English Premier League football club who was desperate to take his father to a crucial league game. Unable to secure tickets via the club, he placed a want ad on the club's unofficial fan site. He quickly received a text from somebody who claimed to have two tickets, which he was selling at face value as he was unable to attend the game. The fan transferred the money but realised that he'd been scammed when, two days before the game, the tickets hadn't arrived despite a couple of texts to the seller. Looking at fan forums, his heart sank when he realised he was one of a number of victims of the same fraudster, who had actually spent time in jail previously for similar crimes ... a habitual offender.

Another way you can fall victim to ticket fraud is to visit a fake website – set up to emulate an authentic one and take payment like an official one, but fraudulent. As well as taking your payment, these sites could also induce you into entering confidential financial information, or infect your computer or mobile device with malware.

If you can't buy tickets from a respectable seller – be it the venue's box office, the promoter or an authentic ticket reseller site – it really isn't worth the risk.

1.5

SOME OTHER COMMONPLACE FRAUD TYPES

Where do I begin?

I both embrace and celebrate the internet for the everyday things it enables us to do, I hope you do too. Sometimes, it's easy to take for granted what we can do so easily and quickly online, and with so much choice: from our weekly shopping to finding love, applying for a driving licence to watching your favourite TV box set. Or simply keeping in touch with friends and family.

But (isn't there always a 'but'?) ... the internet has become a rich grazing ground for the criminal element, as they can reach so many more people with so many more believable scams in a relatively unregulated environment. Can cyber experts and law enforcement stay one step ahead? We certainly have the best minds and some fantastic technology, but there are two snags: the unbounded deviousness and lack of moral compass of scammers, and our own online behaviours.

As a result, it seems that with everything you do online, there's a risk of being defrauded, having your identity stolen or putting yourself in the firing line for some kind of abuse.

Here, I'm going to briefly list some of the most commonplace fraud types that I come across in my everyday work in cybersecurity advice, outline how they come about and how you can avoid them. Understandably, there are similarities between all of them, as all are different ways for criminals to steal your money or identity ... or both.

Counterfeit goods

Consumer demand for designer clothing and accessories, sports club-branded apparel and the latest phones, electrical beauty products and other sought-after goods has fuelled the increase in counterfeit goods.

You've always been able to buy fakes from market stalls, and traditionally, many people chose a particular holiday destination purely for the range of counterfeit shoes and handbags on offer. Now, as with many things, the internet has made it possible for counterfeiters and their distributors to advertise and sell goods to many more people, in their own country or anywhere in the world.

Buying counterfeit goods is definitely not to be recommended. They will almost certainly be of inferior quality: clothes may fade or shrink prematurely after a few wash cycles, handbags may fall apart. Buying fakes can put you in danger too, with garments not meeting flame retardant requirements and electrical goods exploding. Yes, it happens. Another major consideration is that by buying counterfeit goods, you're putting in jeopardy the businesses that manufacture and market the real deal, as well as the livelihoods of the people that work for them. The goods could also have been produced using slave , child or otherwise exploited labour.

It has been known for the confidential details of people buying from counterfeit goods websites to be used and passed on to email spammers, meaning they receive an endless flood of unwanted emails from some pretty nefarious senders. In a number of cases, buyers have been set up as unwitting owners of new websites set up by counterfeiters, only to realise what's happened when they have been contacted by the police.

For all of these reasons, I advise that you never knowingly buy counterfeit goods.

So how can you tell the difference, when you're shopping online? Sometimes it's difficult, with sellers' descriptions and fraudulent websites being highly convincing. If you're visiting a website in response to a social media post, text or email – or an ad on a selling noticeboard or auction site – ask yourself why the goods are being advertised in this way. Is the price too low? Does the website have the right address, spelled the correct way? Is it professional, is the grammar correct? Have you read reviews or taken recommendations? Whether the goods are for you or bought as a gift, the results can only be negative, to one degree or another.

Buying and selling vehicles

One could write an entire book on buying and selling vehicles, in fact many people have. In such a book, the advice would extend well beyond the online aspects. If you're buying: checking the documents and making sure it's not two written-off cars welded together, for example. If you're selling: not allowing solo test drives and making sure you have cleared payment before handing over the keys. However, the book you're reading here focuses on the internet, so I'll mention some of the aspects of buying and selling that you need to be aware of in the online context.

Bear two things in mind: The majority of people who

buy and sell cars, vans and trucks online are honest and want a fair deal, and these days, there's rarely such a thing as a bargain. I sit on a body in the UK comprising the main vehicle buying/selling online media, along with representatives from law enforcement, fraud prevention and consumer protection bodies. We hold quarterly meetings to advise on new types of fraud and share best practice, and I never leave without being amazed at the latest, often complex scams doing the rounds.

If you're buying, you do need to be careful when you spot a vehicle that catches your eye, before you go to the next stage. As I've said, most advertisers are honest, but some are not …. advertising vehicles that don't exist, asking for an up-front deposit, or a fee to transport the vehicle 'in good faith' to where you are in the country so that you can view it. They're normally based at the other end of the country. Coincidence? I don't think so. Then, there are the ads which are misleading, or downright dishonest. The description of the vehicle's condition may be a far cry from the reality. It may state a lower mileage than that actually travelled, in fact is isn't unusual for a vehicle to have been 'clocked' (mileage adjusted). In a worst-case scenario, you could be buying a car which has been stolen, or written-off and repaired, but unroadworthy.

I recommend that you always view the vehicle for yourself at the seller's premises (whether a private or trade seller), and always have some kind of history check carried out to determine that the mileage is correct, and that the vehicle hasn't been stolen and isn't subject to uncleared finance. This is in addition to viewing the appropriate roadworthiness certificate and checking that the documents presented match the vehicle itself. As I mentioned above, this book is about the online aspects of buying and selling.

Selling online has potential hazards as well. I've heard of fraudsters who, posing as potential purchasers, offer to pay the entire vehicle value via a PayPal or similar account created with false credit card details. Then, there are buyers who request a refundable deposit for completion of the sale and collection of the vehicle. Needless to say, the refund never takes place. Slightly further in the process, there's the age-old problem of payments, such as with forged bankers' cheques or fake escrow services.

The overriding advice to sellers is that you should never be duped into paying any up-front fees to potential buyers, however they are described, and further down the line, never hand over your vehicle keys or documentation until you can confirm that its full value has cleared into your bank account.

Buying medicines

Buying medicines or other healthcare and personal products without a prescription is another thing that's become a whole lot easier since the advent of the internet.

There are many legitimate, licensed online pharmacies where you can have medical prescriptions fulfilled and buy other, over-the-counter drugs, but I'd like to alert you to the dangers of buying from other sources.

The type of counterfeit and unlicensed medicines available online include supposed treatments for a range of conditions as diverse as cancer, diabetes, arthritis and hair loss ... all offered without the need for a prescription or any medical supervision. Plus, the classic that's the topic of many a junk email: male potency pills (and condoms , of course).

Medicines that haven't been licensed for use *have not been tested* for safety or effectiveness either, meaning they could not only be ineffective, but could also pose a serious risk to your health, even with fatal consequences. For example, I recall a raft of reports of people buying unlicensed tanning injections and nasal sprays who became ill from unexpected and unwelcome side-effects including optical disorders and heart problems.

If a medicine or other healthcare product hasn't been regulated, it may have been produced in a dirty factory with no hygiene controls. It may contain ingredients completely irrelevant to the results it claims to achieve. And it may even contain elements which are toxic and potentially fatal: mercury, lead and rat poison have all been identified in various cases over the years and continue to do so.

Most countries have regulatory authorities which regulate the sale and distribution of unlicensed medicines and healthcare products. They tend to work hand-in-hand with law enforcement agencies in order to track down the perpetrators, seize the offending goods and close down the distribution networks – including unlicensed online pharmacies. But, of course, new operations and websites are set up as quickly as old ones are closed down. Another important consequence of buying from such sources is that you could become a victim of payment card or identity fraud or having your email account hacked into.

Therefore, before you even consider buying medicines or healthcare products from any source but a licensed online pharmacy, heed my advice and purchase from authorised channels ... it just isn't worth taking risks when it comes to your and your family's health.

And importantly, if you have purchased medical products that you believe may have been fake – or have any concerns or information that may assist in tracking down the culprits – don't hesitate to contact your country's regulatory authority or the police.

Dating

Romance has always been used as a vehicle to defraud people, but the internet has made it easy for scammers to defraud many more people in more convincing ways ... and with relative anonymity.

Typically, dating fraud (or 'romance fraud' as it's often known) takes place when you've established an online relationship with someone which develops for a while until they tell you that they want to take things further and come and meet you in person, or that they or a relative is very ill. In either case, they can't get their hands on the money they need immediately and ask you to help. This usually starts with small amounts, but the lies and amounts requested steadily increase. Many intelligent and generally savvy people have lost considerable amounts of money – even their life savings and homes – through being taken in. Although dating fraudsters can work alone, they are generally organised crime gangs and your loss is their bread and butter.

Of course, it's doubly traumatic because you've not only lost your money, but also been thwarted in love. My advice is to use reputable dating sites, to carry out a reverse image search on profile pictures to see if you're being 'catfished', and to *always* keep the conversation with your suitor on the site's communication platform rather than being tempted to move to texting, email or some other kind of direct messaging. And however well you think you've come to know the other person, however convincing their story and however desperate you are to develop the relationship, remember that online dating fraud is becoming increasingly commonplace.

Not really to do with fraud, but another word of

warning: if your relationship does progress to the point where you both decide to meet in person, meet in a public place, tell someone where you're going (and who you're meeting) and keep your phone handy. In short when it comes to both online dating and meeting, never be pressured into doing anything you're not comfortable with and think twice before you do.

As I've mentioned, the foregoing section represents just a few examples of how you have to be careful and follow a few simple 'rules' before transacting online. I've chosen these to give you an indication of the diversity with which cybercriminals operate, and that they have no conscience about whom they defraud and how much trauma they cause. Keep it safe!

1.6

COPYCAT WEBSITES

Elsewhere in this book, you'll find a number of references to fake websites … those set up by fraudsters which mimic authentic sites in order to defraud you, capture your confidential information or steal your identity (or all three).

Copycat websites have similarities, but depending on where in the world you live, they may or may not be regarded as illegal. You could say that the motive of the owners of these sites is fraudulent, but in general, you will get the service you ordered without your money or identity being stolen, but you'll end up paying well over the odds for it. So, what is a copycat website?

Have you ever carried out an online search for an official, public-sector supplied product or service, to be presented with a raft of options offering what you're looking for? I'm referring to applying for a driving licence or test, a duplicate birth or marriage certificate, a health card, a passport/visa or even just a fishing licence. They all have one thing in common: there's a fee payable when you apply which is always higher than the fee payable on the official site. Sometimes, the authentic service is actually free.

Somewhere amongst all of these search results will

be the official site, but it's often difficult to distinguish this from the various copycat sites also listed. For a start, the copycat sites are often higher on the search page. They may have similar website addresses to the official site, and similar descriptions. When you've clicked through to the site, it has a similar (if not the same) look and feel to the official one, and even a logo which is close to the real thing.

But it's *not* the real thing. The scam is that you will be invited you to fill in the official-looking application form for the product or service you want, then be ripped off with an inflated price for the service. This is sometimes couched as an 'administration fee', that you're paying the extra for your application to be 'fast-tracked', or that there's some other benefit such as your application being 'reviewed' before submission. Generally, however, your application will be submitted verbatim via exactly the same channels as the official site, so there is no benefit ... except to the bank balances of the copycats.

It isn't uncommon for copycat websites to charge *double the official fee*, and sometimes considerably more. In fact in many cases, there isn't a fee chargeable for the official product or service, but you'll get charged anyway by these sites.

I mentioned above that the legality (or not) of copycat sites is a grey area. That having been said, six people in the UK were given substantial custodial sentences in April 2018 after defrauding the public out of over STG£37 million in one of the largest UK online crime cases brought to court. The group had set up and operated a number of copycat sites which impersonated 11 government services to sell driving tests and licences, passports, visas, birth and death certificates, vehicle road tax discs and the London Congestion Charge.

The way that copycat websites often appear so high up

on search engine pages (such as Google and Bing) is the way any other website achieves it, by paying the search engine for the prominent position. It used to be tricky to tell the difference between an entry that appeared in a high position naturally (or 'organically' in online advertising-speak) and one that had been promoted, but now it's very obvious that an ad is an ad. Most prominent search engines have stopped copycat sites from buying advertisements, but some still slip through the net. Of the copycats that do still appear, some make it quite clear that they are not the official site, whilst with others, this information is hidden away in a small font. I imagine there are still others where this information isn't given at all.

If you do find that you have paid money to a copycat site, it can be very difficult to get a refund, with most operators notoriously reluctant to hand back payments. I suggest you contact the site straight away to cancel your contract and request a refund on the basis that you did not realise that you'd purchased a service that you could have obtained through official channels for less cost, or free. Some sites have terms & conditions which say that refunds will be made against a claim made within a certain time period. Try to avoid calling, however, as you could get charged a premium for doing so (these are the sites that just keep taking).

If you do not receive a refund, you could report the site to your local consumer protection authority or seek professional advice. Further action may not be worth the time or money that the matter takes to pursue, depending on the fee you've paid in the first instance.

Whether you receive a refund or not, you should report the copycat site to the government agency or department which offers the *official* service. It's only from reporting such sites that they can be investigated and closed down. Bear in mind that the proceeds from copycat websites go to fund extravagant lifestyles for their owners at your expense, and in extreme cases, more sinister organised crime such as people trafficking, slavery and terrorism.

My overriding advice is to take your time when looking for the official website. You can normally tell the authentic one if the address is a government (or local authority) one, it carries the official branding and contact details and the costs are cheaper. If for any reason at all you do choose to use an unofficial site (and I can't think why you would after reading this), make sure the payment page is secure by checking that the address begins with 'https://' ('s' is short for 'secure') and that there's a locked padlock in the address panel.

PART TWO

INDIVIDUAL, FAMILIES & COMMUNITIES

By

Maureen Kendal
Director of CyberCare

AN OVERVIEW

To 'conquer the web' is to become empowered to use the internet as a lifelong learner. Emerging technology today is rapidly evolving. To keep in step, we need to evolve and be empowered as active participant learners.

The challenges of the internet are:

1. Being overwhelmed by information overload
2. Making consumer decisions, faced with choices of online products, services and user communities
3. Identifying the way we organise our online knowledge and ensuring it is effective
4. Keeping secure and protected across our IT system
5. Enabling Trust, Consent and Privacy by understanding who we are and what are our digital identities?

Within that context, CyberCare offers cyber security advice and support to individuals, families and communities through empowerment and resilience grounded in technical knowledge. Building on Cyber Essentials, we enable the individual to build up skills in IT lifestyle management. We consider how to protect the individual within families and communities, what are our online digital identities, what are the risks and vulnerabilities. What is cyber abuse, hate and anger? How to protect against serious cyber abuse?

Cyber security advice to individuals needs to offer a comprehensive and systematic support system that protects their IT systems which includes a range of devices, applications and platforms. Support requires a technical understanding of IT systems, how they can be hacked into and how the information held there can be compromised, and moreover, how idiosyncratic people use their IT systems, their smart phones and smart devices such as Smart TV, Games Consoles and household products which are internet enabled, commonly referred to as the Internet of Things – IOT.

The most common hacks for business and organisations are enabled by mis-configuration and intruder threat. This is the same for the individual, families and communities, but here the control is not in the hands of the IT support and service department. IT support and service departments are able to control access and provide clear instructions to their end users. The individual in the community does not have access to a carefully managed IT system with protected access or the IT support of an organisation, and therefore needs to, independently and carefully manage their own IT system and their unique IT lifestyle independently and carefully.

As individuals, we expect to be able to manage our individual lifestyles so that we can flexibly access our smart phones, laptops and internet enables devices. We expect our IT devices to be adaptable across different physical environments – home and out and about – and available 24/7 across our different devices. We expect to access and participate across different social media platforms and yet retain our individual personal identity without compromise or threat. However, we tend to use these platforms and systems sometimes in an unorganised chaotic way. Media, advertising and culture encourage aspirations that are spontaneous, and desire driven. We expect these devices and systems to support our relatively free and easy liberal lifestyles.

2.1

BUILDING RESILIENCE INTO OUR INTERNET LIFESTYLE

Resilience is the capacity to recover quickly from difficult challenges. The National Crime Agency places building resilience in the community as their Key Performance Question 6.[4]. Resilience in the community relies on the interrelationship between government and individuals, families and groups. Individuals need to respect and take responsibility for the protection of lives and ownership of property and information. Often systems go wrong, people make mistakes. People and information become vulnerable to abuse.

In order to build resilience and combat Cyber Risk in our IT lifestyle, we need to understand how our IT systems can be vulnerable and open to risk. If we are not aware of our potential vulnerabilities we cannot protect ourselves or bounce back after attack. To keep our IT systems as safe as possible, we need to assess what, who and where to trust.

Imagine our non-digital world; what does Trust feel like in this non-digital world? We are at home. It's a Sunday, we are relaxed in weekend loafing clothes,

4. The National Crime Agency – Annual Plan 2018-2019. KPQ6. p18.

we place our secret diary, our personal photos, our intimate symbolic objects in our top drawer. We put our valuables somewhere safe, accessible and near us. We hide our most valuable items in a security box, under the floorboards, in a bank vault, or maybe in a not-to-be-used special sock in our sock drawer. Later in the evening we get dressed in our smart casuals and we invite trusted friends over and share a meal or go out for some drinks and tell them a joke or about a funny slightly embarrassing incident or joke. On Monday we go out in our work clothes, we put on our coats, umbrellas, hooded jackets or sunglasses. These clothes and accessories signal our status, our social or religious tribe, the type of work, and they might shield us against the weather. We lock our home, its windows and doors, maybe put on our alarm system. At work or with people we meet in the street or at public events, we may not share our intimate, sensitive or embarrassing images or stories. We make judgements, when and with whom, we share different types of information.

We make decisions on how open or restricted we create our communication boundaries. Our non-digital physical world offers us choices. We base these choices on our perception of trust and identities. We use keys, locations and decoys to hide, obscure or to securely mark and identify valuables. We judge whom we might trust, then decide on what to tell and what not to say. We might reveal unique or sensitive information whilst seeking to belong to a specific group, as part of socialising empathising behaviour – 'I too am like you or I am not like you.' Why do we share sensitive communication? Why do we trust or mis-trust? We trust, love, cherish and empathise with others because, as babies and children, we were able to bond with our care-givers and trust them to love us, feed us and protect us. We trust because we are human. Trust enables us to survive, create and procreate in the physical world. Validating trust and trusted communication channels is essential to being safe online.

Our right to use the internet safely?

Being secure online and mindful of cybersecurity, is now part of human rights and responsibilities[5]. We navigate our way through our lives, balancing our ability to empathise and our ability to make sound judgements. We seek to communicate: to belong to our social or interest group, tribe, geographical region, to understand our narratives. Who are we? What are our values? What are our expectations? What can we contribute to our communities? How can we put bread on the table and shelter over our heads? How can we make relationships and build family structures? However we navigate our worlds, we need to be connected online, locally and globally. Today we cannot be active and contributing citizens without being online. This is a human right. Legally, we are entitled to expect access to the internet and have global reach into an extensive knowledge base. Amber Rudd's announcement in April 2018 indicates that the government is providing a £9 million fund available to law enforcement to tackle those who use the anonymity of online space for illegal activities such as the selling of firearms, drugs, malware and people. £5 million will be used to support the police to establish dedicated cyber crime units. This is a step towards cyber safety. CyberCare's cost assessment of a necessary and significant shift indicates that this is insufficient. A comprehensive approach

5. Declaration of Human Rights Article 27. http://www.unesco.org/culture/culture-sector-knowledge-management-tools/11_InfoSheet_CulturalRights.pdf

needs to encompass cyber education, culture and technology. Requirements are cyber awareness training, early intervention flagging up potential incidents, crisis Intervention and sustainable structures within our communities. This comprehensive approach is needed to keep on top of the cyber challenges that are evolving and emerging.[6]

Being online – Education, Culture, Technology

We need to be educated to make judgements on how to be safe. Culturally, we have social identities, we present social and business selves in specific ways, we need to consider what maybe sensitive information. Technically, to protect ourselves, we may use decoys or safety locks, trusted certificates and personal identities.

We can use education, culture and technology to build an online world which offers ways to trust and empower us. We need to know who to trust and how this can be validated across different scenarios.

IT systems are enabled by many layers within the communication network. As we use the IT system, trusted pathways within each layer need to be validated. Cyber-Education needs to build IT knowledge and skills integrated with roles, responsibilities and citizenship. Cyber-Culture needs to enable dialogue between generations, cultures and other digital divides. Dialogue that promotes caring, sharing, creativity and business exchange yet is protected by legal boundaries. Cyber-Technology can be understood as a systematic, comprehensive framework. IT is not simply a product e.g. iPhone or a community such as Facebook, but is a complex system with access points, layers, components, connectivity and code. This three-pronged approach of

---

6. cybercare.org.uk, April 2018;
https://www.enterprisetimes.co.uk/2018/04/12/amber-rudd-announces-crackdown-on-dark-web

education, culture and technology, underpins specialist advice and government intervention. The approach is not new; ten years ago, the Bryon Review sought to safeguard children in the online environment, [7] through improved legal regulation, education, classification reform and technical safety settings.

If we use essential safety guidelines, how safe are we?

Fear of using the internet stems from a basic lack of knowledge, from being a target of a common scam or from unusual or abusive targeted malicious personalised attacks.

There are common safeguards which the public are advised to take on board. The National Centre for Cybersecurity offers online resources aimed at business users – Cyber Essentials. [8]

These are:
1. Firewalls
2. Security settings
3. Controlled access
4. Protection against malware
5. Updating your devices

Their guides for small business users advocate these five steps. [9] The hope is that this awareness will filter down from small business users to the individual, families and the communities. In many cases this may occur, but the majority of individuals at home and out and about are still at risk. For households, families and individual users, we advocate these Cyber Essentials.

---

7. The Bryon Review, June 2008.
8. https://www.cyberessentials.ncsc.gov.uk.
9. Cyber Security Small Business Guide and Infographic, www.ncsc.gov.uk/small business. 2017

Cyber Essentials

1. Back up
2. Update all devices and software and protect against malware using anti-virus software
3. Control access by using passwords and authentication and where possible firewalls
4. Use closed and secured networks
5. Beware of scams, spoofing, spam and phishing.

Anti-virus software protects about 30-40% of known hacks. 60-70% of reported cybercrime can be minimised by using these Cyber Security Essentials. However, 20% of hacks are more complex to defend and protect. Abusive targeted malicious personalised attacks are difficult complex challenges and account for only 0.5-2.5% of all reported hacks.

Most individuals, most of the time, if they use these common Cyber Security Essentials, can use the internet safely without fear.

2.2

ONLINE IDENTITY AND IT LIFESTYLE

We buy IT devices and systems. We have online identities. Our homes, families and communities are online. IT lifestyle management is crucial. Everyone needs to use the internet safely. Using computers, smartphones, internet enabled TVs and IT enabled devices, is not a simple matter of 'turn on and play', although suppliers would like their consumers to believe this. We all need to manage our IT lifestyle. The benefits of being connected online everywhere, 24/7, are enormous and have revolutionised our lives, which surpass the challenges. Today our challenges are information overload and cyber safety. As individuals, we can conquer the web so we can be empowered if we go offline we become diminished.

Using your connected technology devices safely, relies on a certain amount of understanding and awareness of its many layers of vulnerability. To make an informed consumer decision, you should go deeper than following a glossy advertising campaign or keeping up with your friends. This section will explain your home IT infrastructure and its many layers and what you can do to protect yourselves against the risk of attack. Also this section will cover the decisions we make when we purchase our IT devices; the types of online identities we create; how we manage and secure our homes, families and communities when we are online and lastly how we can combat cyber abuse.

In this section we will explore the following:

1. Consumer Choice: First, we will consider how best to protect the individual against cyber-attack by considering consumer options, common challenges, common risks and how to combat these challenges and risks.

2. Levels of an IT system: Secondly, we will consider how to use trust and protective measures to protect across the several layers of IT systems. Each layer can allow or block access and entry. We need to provide methods of testing who and what to let in, at each layer. Only then can we comprehensively and systematically protect against risk and minimise vulnerabilities.

3. Our Online Identity: Thirdly, we will consider who we are online, and what we are doing online? What are our identities and roles? How do we protect our different types of activities?

4. Our Homes, Families and Communities Online: Fourthly, we will offer ways you can protect your families through ways to manage your IT lifestyle, facilitating all generations within the family to enhance everyone's wellbeing online.

5. Cyber Abuse, Hate and Anger. Practical Solutions: What is going on? How does this affect the lives of individual victims, women, children, vulnerable adults and all types of victims? Practical solutions for serious cyber abuse.

Consumer choices when going on or how to go online

Choosing a laptop or smart phone or tablet for individuals in a family is a familiar discussion. 50% of young people go on to higher education, and although computer labs are provided at universities and colleges, most students seek to purchase their own laptop so as to be capable to study, communicate and be entertained everywhere anytime. Most individuals tend to use a smartphone for communication, camera, travel maps, media and entertainment, shopping and socialising.

Currently top of the smart phones are Samsung's Galaxy S8, Galaxy Note 8, Apple's iPhone X, iPhone 8, Google's Pixel 2 and Pixel 2 XL; OnePlus 5T, Essential Phone, LG G6, LGV30, Huawei Mate 9, 10 ProSony Xperia XZ, premium Moto 5G, Honor 9, HTU U11.[10]

Currently top of the social range of laptops are Apple Mac, Samsung, Microsoft Surface. Cheaper solutions are HP, Acer, Asus, Lenovo.[11]

What support is offered for the customer?

Apple retail stores offer face to face tutorials, IT support for their products on demand face to face and online. All should offer operating systems updating service. To minimise cyber hacks and to optimise systems, operating systems and all software should be regularly updated, and any vulnerabilities patched, repaired or eliminated. All devices are likely to be targeted by cyber criminals by new releases of cyber hacking methods, viruses, worms, trojans, social engineering phishing or ransomware emails, but how frequently and effectively will the software developers be able to offer you updated software

---

10. https://www.t3.com/features/best-smartphone, https://www.techradar.com/news/best-phone, https://www.techadvisor.co.uk/test-centre/mobile-phone/best-phone-2018-3210667/
11. https://www.cnet.com/topics/laptops/best-laptops/, https://www.pcworld.co.uk/gbuk/computing/laptops/laptops/703_7006_70006_xx_xx/1_20/rating-desc/xx-criteria.html, https://www.apple.com/uk/mac/

that corrects and patches your device and IT system, thus offering you increased protection?

Tips on choosing a laptop or smartphone

Choice is continually evolving across this competitive market. You need to consider several features when making a choice.

1. Cost and durability.
2. PC vs Mac. Note that Mac comes bundled with integrated software, regular software updates, face to face or online support, service and help at Apple Stores and offers seamless integration between iPhones, iPad, iCloud and Mac laptops.
3. Servicing and support options, Technical Support Forums, how to restore your operating systems, Dynamic-Link Library (DLL) files, or allocate memory or clean up or restore damaged software or hardware, allocate C drive for processing and other drives for storage.
4. Data Storage and Share, Back up methods – external hard drive and Cloud Drives (Dropbox, iCloud, Google Drive, OneDrive, AWS – Amazon Web Services).
5. Functions and features such as whether you need a lightweight or portable device.
6. Given your needs, e.g. the eLearning platform at your university, your work or leisure or social media platform – consider which browsers are supported by your required app or platforms, and is this browser supported by your device? All apps and platforms you are likely to use – should be regularly supported by the operating system of your computer or device.
7. If you are offered a second-hand device – support

maybe not be offered by the supplier. Best to purchase a new computer or device. If you do get a second-hand hardware device (computer, smart phone, physical product), check the previous owner was the legal and registered owner, you must be able re-register it with the suppliers. Computers and IT devices have a limited shelf life, maybe maximum 5 years at best.

8. Software suppliers. Register your ownership with your name with major software suppliers (Microsoft Windows, Apple, Adobe, Media Channels etc.). Operating systems and all software should be regularly updated.

9. There has been vast improvement in interoperability between operating systems and apps – iOS or Android ecosystem (Apple iCloud and devices, Microsoft Office and Cloud). Google apps are operable on Apple iPhone while Samsung is competing by offering similar products on Samsung devices. For ease of use – use one tech eco system across your devices (phone, laptop, tablet).

10. Possible problems may include unwanted Adware, Browser Hijackers, incorrect time and date, Windows Updates (if you use windows), unwanted apps.

11. Check latest security breaches and hacks on your shortlist of possible devices. How often and how effective does your computer supplier send their customers information on updated systems, patches and bug fixes? [12]

12. New features such as touchscreens on laptops may not be as effective as touch screens on smart phones. Be aware of new features which glitter but have little real benefit.

12. https://thehackernews.com/search/label/Lenovo%20Backdoor%20Malware, https://thehackernews.com/search/label/Apple%20MacBook, https://www.wired.com/2016/05/2036876 https://www.securityweek.com/asus-router-flaws-disclosed-several-researchers

How to tackle common challenges when using laptops, devices, smart phones

Common challenges are:

- slow processing
- information overload (if not automatically allocated – memory allocation)
- lack of organisation of folders and labelling of files
- creating a WLAN or network in your home – securing your IT system from the moment you own a device, accessing the network to go online, to using application and storing and sharing confidential data
- Slow computers – PC using Microsoft Windows. Tip: To clear it, click on the start button, in the search field, type: msconfig and then go to the "Startup" tab. You don't want to unmark anything that is a Microsoft process. What you should look for are names like Google Update, AdobeAAMUpdater, Steam Client Bootstrapper, Pando Media Booster, and Spotify. These can be unchecked, to ensure your PC runs faster. Slow computers can be an indication of spyware, remote access, mis use or incorrect configuration.

How to tackle information overload

Emails: To clear unwanted emails, enable junk mail filtering and to trash junk regularly, use the Flagging features to organise and prioritise.

Twitter: Use different twitter accounts for different personas or roles. Use Buffer or a scheduling app to present yourself or your organisation at up and coming meetings, events and activities. Be relevant when communicating in social media channels. Avoid strong emotive language or tit for tat abusive language. Empathise with its audience and think about what it may achieve, benefits and consequences. Media personalities may use tit for tat abusive or emotive language to mask and create a decoy for political developments. Most users are likely to require purposeful and relevant communication bites that are enable growth and development or offer social or business value.

What kind of user are you? What kind of logical system do you use? Some systems are like a filing cabinet, they use named nested folders and files. Other systems are conceived of a mind map with arrows linking themes and ideas across documents, media and images. Users are often either logical or creative thinkers and therefore use different and unique systems to store their online assets, information and images. Often creative and divergent thinkers are working with inter-connecting ideas, images and information that cross over from one folder to the next because their perception is that their material maybe relevant for several projects.

Searching on the Web uses algorithms, with many using semantic or linguistic associations, frequency, probability and purchasing behaviour to offer you useful web hyper-links related to your search. In a sense, the web is both a divergent and hierarchal 'thinker'. Some users are both logical and creative thinkers and they tend to use different types of logical associations. Your online IT system should be structured to work best with your unique way of thinking. Your unique way of thinking and storing is valuable, keep this secured.

Here are some basic tips that may help you create an online system that works best for you.

- Thinking logically and arranging your material into folders and nested folders can be an advantage.
- Tagging folders with colours can help searching for themes and projects.
- Using Search Functions effectively – by restricting your vocabulary to common search words within a coherent framework across all your documents.
- Creating a list of search words that cross over all your types of projects by drawing a mind map can help.
- Make use of your applications that enable Visual Image and Screenshot capture, Notes, Documents, Spreadsheets and Presentations with search functions for cross referencing.
- Create your own templates so you can duplicate recurring information
- Make use of smart folders and mailboxes. If secured and correctly configured make use of cloud systems across compatible systems so that your information and your unique information system – reflecting the way you think – is backed up and accessible across all your devices.

Understanding how you think, whether you use divergent connections and hierarchical folder structures or both, can help you think about keeping yourself secure. Our approach is to secure and protect you using both a systematic comprehensive review of your IT system in conjunction with your divergent, creative and unique user behaviour, how you use the web, who you are in your online world and what type of user you are.

How to choose a network
Networks connect the home both to the outside world and between devices within the home. Networks provide internet access, the ability to share files and

printers, and home entertainment. You may need a hub, switch or router. WLAN – offers a Wireless Local Area Network (WLAN). When you purchase services from an Internet Service Provider (ISP), check their reputation and whether they send you regular updated router hubs. Our research indicates that there is significant difference in the quality of service and functionality across ISP services. Cheapest is not the best. Some provide routers which offer features that can allow your router to be customised to maximise security. You are advised to purchase flexible contracts, so you can change provider if they fail to provide you with a safe and customisable service. You are advised to use a router and/or app that enables you to see, identify and block any device using your Wi Fi and network at any time. Only you and your trusted users in your home should have access. All routers should be regularly re-set with new passwords and physical access to the router restricted to trusted users.

2.3

SECURE AND PROTECT

CYBER ESSENTIALS PLUS

How to combat common risks

BACK UP: Ensure you have safe back up and regular method to back up, using disconnected external drive and an online back-up service.

UPDATE: Ensure you regularly update your IT system, devices, operating system, software applications and protect against Malware by using anti-virus software. Do not use old IT devices and operating systems that cannot be updated and are not supported by the manufacturer.

CONTROL ACCESS: by using passwords, passcodes, two-factor or multi-factor verification and authentication methods. and security features across all your IT system, on all devices and at each level. Protect access by never sharing passwords or pins or passcodes. Use Firewalls where possible.

USE SECURED NETWORKS: Use unsecured open networks with caution; Secure or lock down your home networks.

BEWARE OF SCAMS: spoofing, spam and phishing. Don't give your sensitive, financial and confidential information to non-trusted parties. Sometimes, even although you have taken these common precautions, these are not enough, your IT system and devices are being hacked or you suspect your information and media is not secure. How can you seek help and obtain support?

The most common challenges are:

- Intruder threat – someone accessing your IT system and devices who is not trusted and may threaten you and your IT system or give access to someone who is a potential threat.
- Security settings and products – that protect any one of the levels in your IT system – are not appropriately configured.
- Who can you trust? Should you be trusting them?

Protecting yourself is not a one stop solution. No Anti-Virus product will protect your online presence 100% of the time. Protecting ourselves online requires a cultural and educational mindset as well as taking sensible technical precautions. Everyone needs to be in control of their own IT lifestyle management to prevent the majority of cyber abuse incidents.

Running a home or a work office that provides a nurturing environment for the family or productive environment for a workforce, requires management skills. Imagine an ideal home that offers enough order and organisation so that each individual can find their things and maintain a level of hygiene and have a place to eat, sleep, play and study. On the other hand a home needs to have enough flexibility and relaxed atmosphere to enable learning and creativity. Likewise, the management of an IT system, computers and devices, needs to offer structure and order as well as flexibility and fluid access. How do we manage our IT systems to achieve this balance between control and flexibility?

What does trust mean? Who might we trust? How can we create and manage Trusted Access on several parallel levels of our IT system? Below we will identify each of these levels and assess ways to manage access.

Who might be an untrusted intruder? Often in our work at CyberCare, individuals have trusted a loved one or family members and the relationships goes wrong or ends. One of the individuals in the relationship now uses their 'trusted' status to spy or harass the other partner by continuing to access the private network, cloud, social media and/or devices. Sometimes an 'unknown' intruder turns out to be a previous employee, or 'friend', that still has access to the IT systems and devices. Often children, who are friends of the children in the family, have been playing together on computer games or online media, and inadvertently or without awareness, may pass on Wi-Fi passwords to people who are not trustworthy. Sometimes a 'friend' or a shop worker may indicate that they can support you with their IT skills, but in fact they create an opening for a vulnerability.

Which levels of your IT system may not be appropriately configured and need to be locked down, only allowing you access? Below we will identify each level, and how they can be configured to lock them down against vulnerability.

Protect across all the levels of an IT system

There is not just one device through which you are accessed. To share and exchange information and media about you, your data and online presence, you are not only using an App or a website, you are using an IT system with several levels.

IT systems or media applications through which we share, and exchange information are built on several levels, or layers of electronic transport. At each of these levels, there are ways to either allow in or to shut out our unwanted access. Control over this semi-porous system is crucial. I use a metaphor of a bath with holes in. Each hole needs to be plugged or patched, otherwise the water will drain out. For example, clients with serious and persistent malicious perpetrators, have changed their email account and password, several times over many years but they continue to use open networks and an unprotected router.

How do we monitor these borders? Who will we let in to our online spaces? In our offline lives we live behind locked doors, private spaces but also move in public areas. Our online world needs to be managed with selective access, with different personas for our online identities.

Our IT system functions using several technology levels. We can secure our IT system at each of these levels. At each level we need to secure its borders. We need to establish a method of verifying Trust and Identity at each level.

At CyberCare, our current diagnostic system is based on several levels:

- Ownership and trusted identities
- Access, the perimeter and ports
- Protocols and the Internet of Things
- Clouds, Servers, Drives, Backup
- Software – Operating systems, Browsers, Applications
- Financial applications, Encryption

What is selective and controlled access?

Let's consider selective and controlled access is like a series of doors, with a choice of locks and keys to open them. How do we use these 'Doors' to guard and lock access to our online world? Firstly, we need to consider each technology level in turn. You'll need to assess the risks of a specific set up and situation. IT products can be configured to enable access for each individual users and which level they can access. This can be dependent on status, hierarchy or trust.

What you need to know about Ownership

- You need to own your own devices – laptops, smart phones and internet enabled products
- Register the devices with the product provider
- Do not use second hand devices or devices from untrusted sources
- Ensure your device only gives access to you. Enable controls such as passwords, passcodes and pins to only give you access
- Change your access identity regularly. If you re-use Passwords, take advice from the NCSC guidelines for 'Living with password re-use'[13]
- Create passwords which use a long combination of random words.[14] Advice on how to use passwords changes so ensure you are up to date with the latest advice[15]
- Only use your devices within a secured and trusted network

13. https://www.ncsc.gov.uk/blog/identity-and-passwords, August 2017
14. https://www.ncsc.gov.uk/blog-post/three-random-words-or-thinkrandom-0
15. http://www.dailymail.co.uk/sciencetech/article-4771194/The-man-responsible-passwords-says-advice-WRONG.html
https://www.ncsc.gov.uk/blog/sociotechnical-security
https://www.ncsc.gov.uk/blog-post/living-password-re-use

Restrict your use of open networks or use open networks sparingly. If you feel that your devices are being at risk or may be compromised by a perpetrator, do not use your devices in Open Networks or Networks where you suspect your perpetrator may have access.

- Do not use your devices in Open Networks or Networks where you suspect your perpetrator may have access
- Do not share your WiFi router with any untrusted user
- Biometric authentication such as fingerprints, facial recognition can be hacked using spoofing through 3D printing, and simulation modelling techniques[16] [17]

What you need to know about your network and its ports

You need to consider how your devices are connecting to the internet network. There are several points of risk and vulnerability as internet channels come in to your home via the optic fibre cables and your router. Likewise there is risk even if you are accessing your internet connection via any wireless service directly, such as through a portable wireless Wi-Fi hotspot or a dongle. The advantage is that there maybe no software to install and you can connect multiple devices at the same time easily. However there will be methods of hacking into your system although receiving data from a wireless

16. 2017, https://www.wired.com/story/iphone-x-faceid-security/
17. biometric authentication and facial recognition software
https://www.ifsecglobal.com/biometric-security-systems-guide-devices-fingerprint-scanners-facial-recognition/
Modelling Suspects' Faces Using DNA From Crime Scenes.
https://www.popsci.com/new-service-reverse-engineers-faces-dna-samples-crime-scenes
How to hack fingerprint biometrics?
https://www.networkworld.com/article/2293129/data-center/data-center-120606-10-ways-to-beat-fingerprint-biometrics.html#slide1

service direct into your devices might be relatively more secure option. In addition it can cost more. You will also need to set up a key to lock down access through Security Access points.[18] All services have points of vulnerabilities at their perimeter. There will always be ways in to access your network, you need to minimise this risk.

Secure your home Wi Fi, network and its access points. Ensure other people outside your trusted circle of family or friends cannot access or discover your network. You can monitor any unknown or unwanted access to your network by using IT products such as Fing, FingBox or Wireshark. Make friends with your Router, take time to get to know its settings and enable its configuration options. You need to be able to set up and monitor the advanced settings on your Router; to reset and override the password by accessing the physical router.

Hints and Tips to secure your router: If you are likely to be targeted – set up your physical router in a hidden location. You can set up the latest protection mode (e.g. WPA, WPA, AES, 2) or you can set up a Firewall. You can use your Toolbox features. It is possible to split channels to offer a choice of different router channels, each with different passwords for different sets of users to use within your home. You may hide your Router credentials for further protection. It is recommended that you may disable the WPS and UPnP features. If you enable Wireless Mac Filtering, each port can be linked to a specific device.

What you need to know about Protocols

1. Many families and households have internet en-abled household products, otherwise known as

---

18. https://www.vodafone.co.uk/shop/mobile-broadband/dongles-and-mobile-wi-fi/

the Internet of Things – IOT. Each item is internet enabled through using a stack of protocols – this is a communication network hand shake or form of structured conversation.

2. Protocols enable datelines that run above the physical layer. Each internet host is identified by a unique IPv4 address and now a new set of unique IPv6 addresses have been introduced to cope with the increased use of the Internet. There can be vulnerabilities created by mis-configurations across these stacks of protocols. 'Without careful planning, you could accidentally run both IPv4 and IPv6, nullifying the security you set up around either protocol.'[19] IPv6 can run end-to-end encryption. Widespread adoption of IPv6 will therefore make man-in-the-middle attacks significantly more difficult. IPv6 makes the redirection of traffic very hard. This added security depends entirely on proper design and implementation, and the more complex and flexible infrastructure of IPv6 makes for more work. Nevertheless, if properly configured, IPv6 networking will be significantly more secure than its predecessor.

3. The problems with IPv6 – There is widespread malware with IPv6-based command-and-control capabilities. So, if your server enables IPv6 by default but your firewall doesn't, there can be more abuse for malicious ends. Proper deployment and configuration is crucial. Moreover, the Snowden revelations have shocked the Internet community and the Internet Engineering Task Force that manages the standardisation of Internet proto-

---

19. https://www.sophos.com/en-us/security-news-trends/security-trends/why-switch-to-ipv6.aspx
https://www.computerweekly.com/feature/IPv6-The-security-risks-to-business
https://www.netswitch.net/the-major-trends-that-will-redefine-network-security-in-2014-2/
Computer Networking: Principles, Protocols and Practice, Textbook by Olivier Bonaventure

cols identified a need to develop new protocols.[20] There are potential vulnerabilities throughout the stacks of protocols that underpin the internet's transmission system.

Where does that leave the individual user in a home who uses IT without a firewall or a VPN, with a range of internet enabled devices with a range of IPV4 and IPV6 protocols?

We would advise you to make a log of all internet enabled products and items in your home and check their security settings and security reputation. Check that you are not using products or IT systems with an incorrectly configured combination of IPv4 and IPv6 protocols. Smart products, from meters, to kettles, TVs, watches, music speakers, toys, games, dolls, and lawn mowers, may increase your vulnerability especially if you are being specifically targeted by malicious attack.[21]

What are Servers?

A computer that runs one or several server programs that connects up a network is known as a host server in a network.

20. https://www.ietf.org/about/
https://www.w3.org/People/Frystyk/thesis/Tcplp.html
21. Internet enabled TV; https://devices.netflix.com/en/recommendedtv/2017/ Samsung, Song, LG,
Internet enabled watches; http://www.goldsmiths.co.uk/c/Brands/TAG-Heuer/TAG-Heuer-Connected/
Internet enabled wireless music devices and speakers; https://www.johnlewis.com/browse/electricals/hi-fi-audio-speakers/speakers/Internet enabled and robotic audio talking or listening toys and dolls ; My Friend Cayla and I-Que Intelligent Robot as 'spy toys' ; http://www.dailymail.co.uk/sciencetech/article-4006310/Are-kids-internet-connected-toys-used-spy-Claims-hi-tech-gadgets-fail-protect-privacy.html#ixzz4rM7mBAhy
Robotic lawn mowers: http://www.lawnbotts.com/lawnbott LawnBott_LB200EL_Robotic_Lawn_Mower.html
https://www.pentestpartners.com/security-blog/author/ken-munro/

What are Clouds?

Cloud computing is a network of remote servers hosted on the Internet to store, manage, and process data, rather than a local server or a personal computer.

What is Back Up?

A back up drive must be physically separate and not linked to network except when backing up, such as an external USB drive or USB pen. IT lifestyle management for individuals needs to include a continuity and disaster recovery plan. In practice, what are the backup arrangements for your data, photo archive, emails, contact details, calendar? Are you backing up your data in the system backed up using an external drive and by an iCloud, Dropbox, One Drive, Google Drive? Is the backup external drive kept separate from the networked system? As in a business, the implications of any cyber-attack need to be considered. The individual, family and household need to put into place a continuity and disaster recovery plan that works for their lifestyle and their needs.

What are the vulnerabilities using Cloud Computing?

Any cloud or server with crucial and sensitive and valuable data requires a good firewall and/or physical separation. Like expensive jewellery, do not leave your sensitive data out for thieves to take. Need to assess what might be valuable to others? Sensitive data which has value to potential thieves, fraudsters or malicious intruders, needs to be protected, perhaps in a separate external drive or on another laptop kept in a double layered shielding protective bag that blocks all major signals.

Families often use shared Clouds like iCloud and/or

shared access keys, or passwords. IT lifestyle management for a family necessitates mutually agreed rules that seek to protect the family network. These agreed rules can be crucial to safety and wellbeing, particularly individuals under threat, they need to be in control of who has access to their IT communication network. In a family where there is or has been domestic abuse or coercive control, children may be shared, go between and/or live with the client and then visit the perpetrator. When they visit the perpetrator-parent, they might take with them and share their IT devices, phones and games. This enables an IT savvy perpetrator to access the client's network.

We often find that our clients have multiple and/or hacked iClouds. Often, we find that their email has been added to an iCloud business account through social engineering. This enables the perpetrator to track and monitor the clients' online communications and geo-locators. At CyberCare we ensure that the Apple ID and their iCloud is completely separated from a suspected or alleged perpetrator's iCloud and any apps with tracking functions.

Where are the vulnerabilities when using servers, clouds, remote networks?

Many commonly used services such as Office 365, Google, Dropbox, and Salesforce are all cloud apps. Using IoT in conjunction with the cloud servers enable complex cyber crime. Some examples include Spiral Toys' CloudPets, which are soft toys that allow children and their parents to exchange recorded messages over the internet. The company stored customer data in an unprotected MongoDB that was easy to discover online. The access and exposure of Hillary Clinton's campaign chief John Podesta Gmail's account, was facilitated through the use of cloud services. Attackers used social engineering to acquire the password for John Podesta's Gmail. The DDoS attack against Dyn's domain name system impacted access to a range of sites in parts of the U.S. including PayPal, Twitter, Reddit, GitHub, Amazon, Netflix, Spotify.

How to maximise safety in the cloud?

Disconnect and Back Up. Protect by a back-up to a physical storage device, such as a USB or a server somewhere. Bear in mind that any ransomware on a system could look around at what drives are connected and encrypt or destroy data there.

Hints and Tips to ensure secure Clouds and Systems:

1. Watch out for any updates or patches issued for any open source software you use.
2. Software updates will frequently include patches for newly discovered security vulnerabilities that could be exploited by attackers.
3. Ensure that the cloud service you use regularly backs up your files to ensure you can replace them should you become a victim of ransomware.
4. Implement regular backups.
5. Organise your information so that you know what and where your information, photos, media, financial, household information is being stored on cloud services. Avoid chaotic systems, organise your family information into labelled folders and a file system that the users understand. Avoid dumping all your files on the desktop with no file structure. Use commonly shared keywords to enable quick search and access.

Software

What are Applications?

An application program is a computer program designed to perform a group of coordinated functions, tasks, or activities for the benefit of the user. Examples of an application include a word processor (MS Word, iOS Pages), a spreadsheet (MS Excel, Google Sheets, iOS Numbers), a web browser (Safari, Chrome, Internet Explorer), a media player (YouTube), a computer game (MineCraft), a photo editor (Adobe Photoshop), or a search engine (Google, Yahoo, Bing, Duckduckgo).

What is an API?

API application programming interfaces enable developers to use technology interface to build applications. By abstracting the underlying structure and only exposing objects or actions the developer needs, an API simplifies programming. An API can be used by the developer without requiring that the developer understands the file system operations occurring behind the scenes. Sometimes less skilled developers using APIs can create security vulnerabilities in error.

Using emails – best practice

Safer email providers are likely to be Gmail, Outlook, Zoho, iCloud and privacy-focused Tutanota, and Protonmail. ProtonMail is also accessible on the "hidden" internet using Tor and through VPNs. Mailfence, Countermail also provide safe email services.

Reminder on using passwords

If you re-use Passwords, take advice from the NCSC guidelines for 'Living with password re-use'.[22] Take advice from the NCSC guidelines: create passwords which use a long combination of random words.[23]

Use multi-factor authentication

These factors can be hidden or secret. Do not use factors which everyone uses and knows. When you are setting up multi-factor authentication, you are asked for factors – such as email addresses, phone numbers, secret answers to create your unique two-factor or multi-factor authentication. If you are a likely target, do not use a phone number or email that is publicly available or available on social media. You need to use hidden or secret factors. These are 'keys' you would only give to trusted friends to your online digital 'home'. Do not share these factors.[24].

What you need to know about using email

- *Beware of keylogging software,* this might be hidden on your computer. This could be part of the operating system that sends back data to a computer manufacturer or sent by a hacker.[25]
- Do not leave your mobile devices and computers unguarded. Devices need to be protected with *strong passwords* or biometrics and have no guest accounts or similarly unprotected access allowed. Consider using a physical protector designed to protect against Wi-Fi intrusion.

22. https://www.ncsc.gov.uk/blog/identity-and-passwords, August 2017
23. https://www.ncsc.gov.uk/blog-post/three-random-words-or-thinkrandom-0
24. http://www.techadvisor.co.uk/feature/internet/best-free-email-services-for-2017-3613837/
https://www.lifewire.com/best-secure-email-services-4136763
25. https://thehackernews.com/2015/09/lenovo-laptop-virus.html

- Be vigilant of social engineering. Phishing attempts often *come by email*, instant messages, VoIP or social networking messages and can be very cleverly designed (possibly tailored specifically to you).
- Do not write down or share any passwords. Never make a note of the password that lets you decrypt secure emails you receive. Use different passwords for your email accounts or social networking accounts.
- Assume that, given enough resources, interest or time, it will be possible to hack into your every email account (even encrypted email).
- It may be even "easier" to force, trick or blackmail you so you reveal information directly or grant access to secure email accounts.

To minimise risk:
- Use a strong password. The longer it is, the more secure it will be. Change your password regularly. Do not share your password.
- Set up your security answers. Use answers that are unknown to anyone else. If necessary, create imagined answers. Secret answers need not be real answers, just ones you can remember.
- Set up two step authentication / verification for your email e.g. Gmail. To do this use a phone number that any likely perpetuator does not know. Consider purchasing a new phone or pay as you go phone.
- Use an email that any likely perpetuator will not know. Do not add anyone else you cannot trust or may not trust in the future as your rescue email ID.
- Safer emails may be Tutanova, Protonmail or Gmail with two step authentication.

- Click links only from known and trusted sources, if unsure speak to your known source to check. Always proceed only if you have checked the source of the link.
- Be careful about what you share. Don't reveal sensitive personal information i.e. home address, financial information, phone number, your real date of birth. The more you share the easier it is to have your identity stolen.
- Become familiar with the privacy policies of the email app you use and customise your security and privacy settings.
- Additional security may be gained through physical security tokens and secure key management systems.

How to handle spam, scam mail and phishing

It is recommended to remove spam using 'unsubscribe' options, 'filters' and 'junk' filters. Regularly consider if you want to remove your email from the sender's mail outs by requesting to unsubscribe. Spam wastes time and wastes your life when you can be doing other things. Don't get hooked into Spam. It is easier said than done. If you follow specific interests or groups that arrive by email – Create folders or mailboxes on your Email Account. Use different search settings to identify all emails with specific headers and move them into specific folders. This can be automated using Smart Mailboxes or Smart Folders. Keep a tidy folder structure. Some people prefer a flat folder structure and other prefer a hierarchal structure for their folders. Label your folders with consistent names or colour tags.

Scam emails and phishing are dangerous. Phishing for business users can be minimised by using educational and awareness software products like Polira[26] [27] Recent targets were Fee paying Independent Schools.[28] Government sites like https://www.ukfinance.org.uk/ training_/financial-crime/ seek to train and protect individuals. The government's current campaign is takefive-stopfraud.org.uk. Refer to the section on Financial Applications for advice on avoiding financial scams.

What you need to know about Browsers and Operating Systems

What is a browser? An application that enables the user to access the Web. What are the safer browsers? Safer browsers currently recommended are Chrome, Opera, Safari, Brave, Tor[29]. [30] A browser enables the user to share and retrieve information from the Web. A user-agent is a software application that enables search functions that request access to a web-site. Browsers will use cookies and other tracking methods to customise and personalise your search functions, enabling your searching and shopping internet experiences. However, if you are being tracked by malicious intruders or attackers, ensure you remove your cookies, geo-locators, your browser and cache histories that are integrated and accessible as part of your browser settings.

26. https://www.polira.co.uk
27. https://www.infosecurity-magazine.com/blogs/effective-phishing-assessment/
28. https://www.itgovernance.co.uk/blog/criminal-hackers-targeting-uk-private-schools/
29. https://www.lifewire.com/what-is-a-browser-446234
https://tiptopsecurity.com/what-is-the-most-secure-web-browser/
https://www.cnet.com/uk/news/privacy-browser-brave-tor-trump/
https://www.slant.co/versus/5232/16094/~tor-browser_vs_bravehttps://www.technochops.com/brave-browser-review-2017-heres-experienced-far/2681/
30. Tor is a browser that enables the user entry into the Dark Net - unlicensed free internet highway, IT specialists have advised using Tor if you are a victim of cyber tracking to ensure your anonymity.

To minimise risk:

- Ensure that your browser, operating system, and software are kept up to date with the latest software.
- When using shared computers or devices, check browser settings, clear the cache and the history, remove cookies. Use alternative browsers such as TOR, BRAVE, CHROME. Probably avoid favourite browsers such as IE, Firefox, Safari. Remember to log off when you have finished.

Internet and the Web

Although webpages contain an enormous amount of information, they are not the only way information is shared over the internet. The internet, not the web, is also used for email, instant messages, news groups and file transfers. The web is a large portion of the internet, but it isn't all of it. The Web is the shop window.[31]

Using Social Media

What is social media?

Social media are computer-mediated technologies that facilitate the creation and sharing of information, ideas, career interests and other forms of expression via virtual communities and networks.

Types of social media

Social media apps include Instagram, Facebook, Messenger, WhatsApp, LinkedIn, MeetUps, Pinterest, SnapChat, and Viber.

---

31. https://www.lifewire.com/difference-between-the-internet-and-the-web-2483335

Ways to minimise your risk:

- Use a strong password. The longer it is, the more secure it will be. Change your password regularly.
- Do not share your password.
- Use a different password for each of your social media accounts.
- Set up your security answers. Use answers that are unknown to anyone else. If necessary, create imagined answers. Secret answers need not be real answers, just ones you can remember.
- Set up two step authentication for any social media you use. To do this, use a phone number that any likely perpetuator does not know. Consider purchasing a new phone or pay as you go phone.
- Do not add anyone else you cannot trust or may not trust in the future as your rescue email ID.
- If you have social media apps on your phone, be sure to password protect your device and use your answer phone pin or passcode.
- Be selective with friend requests. If you don't know the person, don't accept their request. It could be a fake account.
- Click links only from known and trusted sources. If you are unsure, speak to your known source and proceed only if you have checked the source of the link is secure.
- Social media accounts are regularly hacked. Look out for language or content that does not sound like something your friend would post.
- Be careful about what you share. Don't reveal sensitive personal information i.e. home address, financial information, phone number, your real date of birth. The more you post the easier it is to have your identity stolen.

- Become familiar with the privacy policies of the social media channels you use and customise your privacy settings to control who sees what.
- When using shared computers or devices, check browser settings, clear the cache and the history, remove cookies.
- If you are or suspect you are being targeted, use alternative browsers such as TOR, BRAVE, CHROME. It is probably best to avoid favourite browsers such as IE, Firefox, and Safari.

Always log off when you're finished using social media. When you re-open and/or reinstall the app, check the privacy settings have not defaulted to Public rather than Private. Settings on some social media such as Facebook have been set to Public Settings by default. Each time the user re-installs the software it enables the Public not the Private settings. The rationale is to encourage public sharing and business advertising revenue. For a cyber abuse victim, using Facebook or any social media without professional cyber security advice is a significant risk.

Remember Facebook is not safe, if you are being targeted by a malicious perpetrator, your friends may be his friends or his friends' friends. For a cyber abused victim, a circle of friends is likely to be linked to a known alleged perpetrator. Seek advice if you are in this situation.

Spyware and tracking software

Spying software is commonly available, sold as parental control apps. These can be used to abuse and track an adult without their consent. Often the victim does not have enough knowledge of IT systems to understand the risks and understand that spyware is commonly used.

Spyware can use a default mechanism, to turn back on geo-locators after those functions have been turned off. Spyware is routinely used to track and monitor the whereabouts of victims of domestic abuse and coercion and victims of so-called 'honour abuse' and modern-day slavery. Elsewhere we have indicated research which indicates that the majority of homicides in cases of known domestic abuse have tracked their victims.

In a family where the members are or were employed as Military and Police with IT knowledge, and there is a situation of domestic abuse with an alleged malicious and coercive perpetrator, we should be aware that this victim's mobile phones might be tracked illegally using professional software with internet enabled trackers e.g. Cellebrite products.

Banking online

What you need to know about financial applications

Listening to and working with families and community agencies, we have identified some of the risks and concerns that affect parents and their children; carers, teachers and young people. Users expect and enjoy the pleasures of an online lifestyle with an IT lifestyle, but this role has responsibilities. This type of challenge offers an opportunity to build trust, communication and confidence between generations. Recommended solutions need to be delivered using a multi-pronged approach through Education, Culture and Technology. Most services and products offer parental controls settings. Families with gamers and social media savvy family members – can consider social and economic controls. Using the new tech banks like Monzo,[32] can enable a parent to give a young person a virtual bankcard that allows measured and controlled pocket

---

32. https://monzo.com/about/

money for online payment to Games and Media Online services. Conversation, consent and shared agreement between family members is crucial.

In our work with victims of domestic abuse or coercion, financial coercion and control is a common aspect. Joint bank or shopping accounts sometimes facilitate tracking and monitoring of adult partners. The culture of using spyware to monitor children's activities and whereabouts can seep into adult relationships where there is mis-trust and suspicion.

Phishing emails can be selectively targeted to specific groups who may be more vulnerable or likely to desire what the criminals are offering or maybe targeting specific open networks locations where further data can be stolen to falsely authenticate access to your bank, shopping, or crypto-currency accounts. Email addresses linked to log in credentials and personal information such as names, addresses and date of birth can be sourced and bought by criminals on the Dark Net. Financial scams include 'criminals promising romance',[33] stolen credit cards,[34] stolen email identities from Yahoo,[35] Hotmail and Gmail, and stolen login credentials from Microsoft, Google, Yahoo,[36] Report any scams to Action Fraud.[37]

Banking online is now 63% of the market.[38] We recommend readers to familiarise themselves with the 'TakeFive-StopFraud' campaign and where possible, for individuals to separate their financial identity from their social and public online identities. The extract

33. https://www.huffingtonpost.co.uk/entry/romance-scams-online-fbi-facebook_us_59414c67e4b0d318548666f9
34. https://jointoken.com/fraud-and-the-dark-web/
35. https://www.independent.co.uk/life-style/gadgets-and-tech/news/yahoo-hack-update-password-email-address-have-i-been-hacked-a7982566.html
36. https://www.independent.co.uk/life-style/gadgets-and-tech/news/gmail-hotmail-yahoo-email-passwords-stolen-hacked-hackers-russia-a7014711.html
37. https://www.actionfraud.police.uk/report_fraud
38. https://www.statista.com/statistics/289081/penetration-of-online-banking-in-great-britain-by-device/

below has been taken from Government advice. We have added some extra information in brackets. The updated website[39] offers an excellent online test to help you spot a hacker targeting you to access your funds https://takefive-stopfraud.org.uk/takethetest/.

In the UK more than 21.5 million people now bank online. There is a high probability that this is a very safe and secure way to access your bank account. Most fraudulent acts with online bank accounts, involves a customer being duped into giving away their user passwords and security information or having their PC infected with spyware. This can be done using remote access and key logging software, designed to steal the information. The two most common attempted scams currently used by online fraudsters are phishing and malware.

Phishing

This is an email that claims to be from your bank (or other organisation) but is sent to you by fraudsters. These emails typically urge you to click on a link that takes you to a fake website, identical to the one you would expect to see. You are then asked to verify or update your personal security information but, by doing so, you are giving your information to the fraudster who has created the fake website. The fraudster then uses the details to access your online bank account and take your money. One easy way to spot phishing emails is that they are usually addressed to "Dear valued customer" instead of using your name. This is because phishing emails are usually sent out at random as the fraudsters only have limited information, such as your email address.

---

39. https://takefive-stopfraud.org.uk, https://takefive-stopfraud.org.uk/takethetest/

Malware (malicious software)

This is a type of virus that can be installed on your computer, without your knowledge. It is capable of monitoring your PC activity, enabling fraudsters to capture your passwords and other personal information. To make sure you don't become a victim of malware, make sure you have up-to-date anti-virus and anti-spyware software installed (30-40% of hacks can be prevented by Anti Malware).

Top tips to prevent online banking fraud (from Government source):

1. Be suspicious of emails which are supposedly from your bank.
2. Never give your login details in full by email or over the phone – your bank will never request these in this way.
3. Make sure your computer has up-to-date anti-virus software and a firewall installed. Consider using anti-spyware software. Download the latest security updates, known as patches, for your browser and for your operating system (e.g. Windows, Apple Operating Systems).
4. Be wary of unsolicited emails requesting personal financial information. Keep passwords and PINs safe; always be wary of unsolicited emails or calls asking you to disclose any personal details or card numbers. Your bank, building society or the police would never contact you to ask you to disclose your PIN.
5. Ensure your browser is set to the highest level of security notification and monitoring. The safety options are not always activated by default when you install your computer (ensure you configure

your computer, do not let any untrusted person configure it for you, if that person becomes untrusted later, immediately seek advice to reconfigure your computer or device).

6. Know who you are dealing with – always access internet banking sites by typing the bank's address into your web browser. Never go to a website from a link in an email and then enter personal details.

7. The login pages of bank websites are secured through an encryption process, so ensure that there is a locked padlock or unbroken key symbol in your browser window when accessing your bank site. The beginning of the bank's internet address will change from 'http' to 'https' when a secure connection is made.

8. Ensure you log off from your online bank account before you shut down, especially if you are accessing your online bank account from a public computer or at an internet cafe.

9. Check your bank statements regularly and thoroughly. If you notice anything irregular on your account, contact your bank as soon as possible. For further advice visit www.banksafeonline.org.uk

Online shopping

The incidence of computer hackers stealing and using cardholder data from retailer websites is low. Similarly, the vast majority of online businesses are honest and legitimate and comply with their obligations to carefully protect and securely dispose of cardholder information. Most internet card fraud involves a criminal obtaining genuine card details in the real world that are then used to shop online (don't share your card details with any untrusted person).

Top tips to avoid online shopping fraud:

1. Be aware that your card details are as valuable as cash, so store your cards securely at all times and try not to let them out of your sight.
2. Sign up to Verified by Visa or MasterCard SecureCode whenever you are given the option whilst shopping online. This involves you registering a password with your card company. By signing up, your card will have an additional level of security that will help prevent you being a victim of online fraud. More information on how to sign up can be found at www.shopsafeonline.org.uk
3. Only shop on secure sites. Before submitting payment details ensure that the locked padlock or unbroken key symbol is showing in your browser (The locked padlock symbol is usually found at the top of the screen if you use Internet Explorer 7 or Firefox 2.). The beginning of the online retailer's internet address will change from 'http' to 'https' when a connection is secure. In some new browsers, such as Internet Explorer 7 and Firefox 2, the address bar may also turn green to indicate that a site has an additional level of security.
4. Never disclose your PIN to anyone and never send it over the internet.
5. Print out your order and keep copies of the retailer's terms and conditions, returns policy, delivery conditions, postal address (not a post office box) and phone number (not a mobile number).
6. Ensure you are fully aware of any payment commitments you are entering, including whether you are instructing a single payment or a series of payments.

7. Consider using a separate credit card specifically for online transactions.

What do you need to know about Encrypted data and Virtual Private Networks?

Data can be compromised using a range of techniques including:

- Remote pervasive monitoring of your IT system – they have access inside your system
- DoS / DDoS: Denial of Service or Distributed Denial of Service – they are flooding your system to make it fail
- Man-in the Middle Attacks – they are accessing your system by receiving the data through a hidden third host without your knowledge

Ways of securing an IT system can use a range of techniques including access and exchange keys, encrypted keys, trusted certificates from known senders, encrypting your data and securing the network by locking it down and limiting its flexibility. Whilst these methods aim to reduce risk, your systems and devices can still be vulnerable. A secure lock down of your IT system, to a specific port or to a specific device severely limits its flexibility.

Home users generally expect a flexible and accessible internet system. For the individual who is the target of malicious attack Virtual Private Networks VPNs can offer a useful means to communicate across a safer network however they can be sluggish and not flexible. Should you use a VPN? Advice indicates that VPN with strong encryption with proper implementation should be used. Avoid VPNs that are primarily based on MD5 or SHA-1 hashing algorithms and PPTP or L2TP/IPSec protocols. Use current versions of OpenVPN (considered extremely secure) and SHA-2. Check which algorithm your VPN uses, refer to the VPN documentation or contact support.[40]

Trusted root certificates can be misused or bogus certificates issued. This can create vulnerabilities. 'An attacker who gets hold of the private key that belongs to a root certificate can generate certificates for his own purposes and sign them with the private key'.[41]

Today many applications offer encryption features. Your applications may indicate that they use some of these encryption technologies: End Point E2EE, PGP (Pretty Good Privacy), however Open Whisper, Signal, and Confide may offer more secure encryption and protocols.[42] Many hacks work by combining social engineering such as manipulating humans to reveal some sensitive data, or a combination of accessing an application with authentication and encryption settings.

Unique identifiers used in Blockchain technology and search and check identify functions in Hash Keys are enabling new developments in Cybersecurity.[43] With these developments it might be conceivable that each data block will be traceable in a transparent system, therefore providing more effective evidence for law enforcement. In the meantime, security breaches can

40. https://www.vpnmentor.com/blog/can-vpns-hacked-take-deeper-look/
41. https://blog.malwarebytes.com/security-world/technology/2017/11/when-you-shouldnt-trust-a-trusted-root-certificate/
https://www.mistralsolutions.com/can-certification-authority-ca-certificates-trusted-any-more/
42. https://www.wired.com/2017/03/wikileaks-cia-hack-signal-encrypted-chat-apps/
43. https://www.csoonline.com/article/3050557/security/is-the-blockchain-good-for-security.html
Blockchain Basics: How is a Hash Different than Encryption - Factom
https://www.factom.com/university/tracks/fundamentals/how-is-a-hash-different-than-encryption
Hash functions accelerate table or database lookup by detecting duplicated records in a large file. Cryptographic hash values are sometimes called (*digital*) *fingerprints, detecting data, or checking for accidental data.*

be inadvertently created by developers using APIs.[44] However the Government has access to the back door. EU plans focus on "three or four options", including legislation and voluntary agreements that would enable police forces to demand the turnover of user data with a swift, reliable response.[45]

44. https://www.thalesesecurity.com/solutions/use-case/data-security-and-encryption/application-level-encryption
45. http://www.itpro.co.uk/security/28394/eu-wants-to-create-backdoors-to-encrypted-social-media-apps
https://www.theguardian.com/technology/2017/jan/13/whatsapp-design-feature-encrypted-messages

2.4

OUR HOMES, OUR FAMILIES, OUR COMMUNITIES

We live in a knowledge driven society. Our tool to search, access and retrieve information is 'Mama Google'. I use 'Mama' in particular to refer to the hope that parents are thought to protect, nurture and cherish their young, empowering the next generation with the sensitive capacity for empathetic and ethical relationships. However, hate, anger, jealousy and violence manifest where there are dysfunctional relationships. On the digital super highway, individuals and families need to have the tools and capability to protect themselves. We would not send our children out on to a busy motorway or even a busy high street without teaching them to cross thread safely, without the capability to cross the road safely, without traffic lights and with no vehicle speeding controls. Even with traffic regulations we would advise any pedestrians to watch out for out of control, drunk or crazy drivers. Likewise, online, we need to understand who is out there and to be able to implement the tools to protect ourselves as we play and work on the digital super highway.

Individuals need to know who has the access key to all the different levels in their IT system, laptops and phones and internet enabled devices. Most importantly who is managing the access keys for each of these levels. Can these people be trusted? What does trust mean? What IT lifestyle management activities need to be implemented? How can families work as a team to offer each other protection and support? One person in charge is not necessarily the best response. Allowing oneself to 'just not being IT savvy' is not an advised option. This threat offers us all an opportunity to be empowered and to work together, sharing IT know how, communication and team skills and to offer mutual support. This opportunity enables inter-generational communication between gamers and grandparents, enabling those who have not traditionally been technically skilled. Enabling those who have traditionally had less economic power and status in families and homes to get technically skilled up – older adults, women and girls. Enabling those who maybe more vulnerable – those with learning difficulties, mental or physical disabilities by building up IT skills management in bite-sized education and in conjunction with their care workers and families.

Online identities

What are our online roles?

In our offline lives we have different roles and relation-ships, and different ways of communicating to others. A grandmother might talk with her grandchild about observing some anti-social behaviour and what behaviour might be acceptable or not. As a professional social carer one might talk to one's work colleagues about the similar unacceptable or anti-social behaviour if it takes place in a work context. On the bus or in the street with a close friend, the same observation might be shared. In each context our exchanges differ depending on our roles, status and type of relationship.

Likewise, online we need our identities to communicate differently using our specific role. Each role has different responsibilities and functions. To protecting our online identity, we need to understand our different roles and the need for different types of identity. Each of your online identities can be protected differently.

The Browser or Viewer or Researcher

Generally, people have a public online identity. They want to browse on public websites, shopping sites, cultural events, community events. The function here is to explore and look and see what is available. Protection is through education about cookies, different types of browsers with a range of security features, using a public or social identity which does not buy, sale, share or exchange sensitive or valuable information. This browser identity is not selling or buying.

The Shopper

This identity is selling, buying and shopping. They want to access to shop. This is a different function. As soon as they become purchasers and get out their 'online wallet', they become more vulnerable. At this point of sale, they are asked to sign in as a purchaser. Protection can be assisted by using a separate trusted and secure identity used only for financial exchange. Banking online offers a range of security applications or physical security plug in as an additional verification factor. Shopping accounts should not be shared. Shared accounts to purchase take away food and other social purchases can lead to compromised accounts. RFID, NFC, and online payment scanning methods can be compromised and hacked, often through sophisticated social engineering scams or close proximity with a second false intruding NFC card.[46] Phishing attacks use social engineering to obtain banking details and elicit payment for false goods or services. Remember the locked icon and https;/ that may indicate that this is likely to be a protected and secure website.

Avatars in virtual worlds

Avatars are the gaming pieces or players within virtual reality and computer gaming platforms and across social media channels. Whilst avatars need not reflect attributes of the real person, they exist as virtual actors or puppets, character personas, game player tokens. Representing and often under the control of their human controller or 'puppet master'.

Sometimes avatars – be they characters in games or virtual actors – are not under human control, but rather are Non-Player Characters NPCs whose role may be to guide, instruct, or fight the player's avatar. NPCs can be coded to elicit prescribed behaviours in response to specific stimuli or instructions, some may be coded as Smart systems to learn from prior 'experience'. Virtual worlds are thus populated by simulated robotic programmed avatars with specific characteristics and coded instructions. Sometimes avatars are created or edited by a real physical person who controls them in MMOs – massively multiplayer online games e.g. Second Life, World of Warcraft and other strategic and creative game platforms.

Benefits include design and development of stra-

---

46. http://securityaffairs.co/wordpress/37667/hacking/nfc-attack-credit-card.html

tegic game play, team-building, capability to design, build and navigate through 3D spatial environments. Empathetic involvement with human scenarios and character identification similar to linear narrative forms such as novels, comics, story-telling. Seven years ago, virtual avatar worlds were understood to be globally connected electronic dolls houses or environments, that miniaturised our real physical world [47]. Today with immersive headsets and new immersive platforms and paint tools e.g. TiltBrush, MasterPieceVR – the scale of the miniature on your digital screen has expanded out to tools and platforms that inhabit 3D human body size centric space. This immersion in 3D virtual augmented worlds enables us to re-inhabit and re-size our physical space with layers of enhanced realities. A gamer's identity is different from his real physical identity. Many users create many different gaming identities that project different attributes of their self. These multi-avatars and immersive identities are part-imagined psychological projections that can seep into our identities as we interact in our physical real world. This 'psychological-cultural-physical self' has imaginatively inhabited cultural artefacts and stories from the first cave painting to contemporary culture and media.

Today there are enhanced risks. The realism and the permeability of the virtual immersive stimulated world poses the question whether the user really understands the difference between the imagined, the real and the virtual. Where lies the agency of self and responsibility? Let's consider these real-life scenarios: a child is playing a game with an internet enabled robotic physical speaking doll. This product fails to offer computer

---

47. 2011 – 'on the making of the Second Life handbook' EVA Electronic Visualisation and Arts, BCS British Computer Society conference- Alan Hudson and Maureen Kendal, contextual reference to business, ethnographical and cultural aspects of Second Life; 2011 – Second Life Handbook – WEISL – Writing Explorations In Second Life. (Hudson and Kendal)

security settings and appropriate configuration. A perpetrator hacks into the doll and game, and through making edits in the code, asks the child to open the locked front door of the real physical house whilst the children's family are asleep. Or a perpetrator talks through the audio speaker of the internet enabled baby monitor[48] and gives persuasive instructions to the child as he pretends to be a game character. Criminal intent can be imagined. The risk of vulnerability is great.

There are real concerns over computer game playing in terms of gaming addiction.[49] Ninety-seven per cent of children play games, 2% become addicted. In addition, there are correlations between children who play aggressive games and their sequential behaviour where they act out the aggression and violence after the game experience. Do children or susceptible young people mimic aggressive and violent behaviour of the gaming characters or have they chosen to play these games because they are inherently aggressive and enjoy the thrust and tumble? Some suggest that these games act cathartically and soak up the child's aggressive energies. Research indicates individuals' psychological profiles of the individual user are likely to have an effect on the user response e.g. on how the game effects the player. Furthermore, pro-social games, where the main aim is to help someone else, have a positive effect on sequential behaviour. Game-playing can be a tool to stimulate and encourage either social or anti-social behaviour.[50] Parents and families could choose to actively harness their consumer power to continue to encourage violent gaming or to advocate pro-social gaming.

48. https://www.independent.co.uk/life-style/gadgets-and-tech/news/baby-monitors-hacked-parents-warned-to-be-vigilant-after-voices-heard-coming-from-speakers-a6843346.html
49. http://www.techaddiction.ca/video-game-addiction.html
50. http://www.educationalneuroscience.org.uk/resources/neuromyth-or-neurofact/violent-video-games-make-children-more-violent/

Socialiser and sharer

As internet users, we share and exchange visual and A/V experiences between families and friends – often through sharing photos, videos and selfies. We use social media channels, texting and tagging features to communicate across friendship groups; larger communities, and even to our 'frien-emies'. Some just post to smaller elite more intimate circles of best friends. Commonly posting pics, text, video, sharing and updating our personal news, life experiences and choices; making social arrangements to meet up in the physical world; researching and documenting educational sources as part of our continual professional development CPD. Chatting and texting online offer us immediate and synchronous flow of 'commenteria'.

Young people sitting in remotely located rooms share opinions on the merits of a new series of say 'Made in Chelsea', or 'Skins', accessed on online media channel, iPlayer or through broadcast channels. This generation are likely to be cyber aware, understanding the risks of disclosing confidential information, or inappropriate material that might be used against them or accessed by potential employers. They may have been taught how to use the internet as professionals or information workers. They are likely to create appropriate email user names and are able to generate hidden 'difficult to trace' online identities if required for illicit, covert purposes or just for fun evenings out. Their social identity can be kept distinct from their professional identity and this distinction would be recommended.

Debater

Our identity as social commenters and debaters offers us the responsibility to imagine the consequences of 'our talk' and 'our debate' into the wider social online communities. This capacity to imagine, enables us to take time to think before we respond immediately to the twitter channels.

As online contributors to forums, political and cultural, users debate, share and exchange immediate responses to the daily news. Social media enables a shift towards a more open democratic society – of commenters and political lobbyists and citizen journalists, facilitating political shifts like the Arab Spring. However, the risk is that without an increase of empathy-education, intellectual and emotional intelligence to leverage these debates, there is always the spectre of mass fascistic tendencies and false news hijacking these new democratic structures inherent social media channels.

In order to mitigate against fascism and a culture of false news, be it leftist state control or rightist capitalist lobbies, government may provide clear ethical leadership to curb unfettered self-interests. With a positive and generous outstretched hand, Media and IT moguls may work with government to offer online communities of users, business services with embedded values of compassion and acts of social responsibility.

Creatives, collaborators, collectors

User generated content is made by creatives, the maker community, from hobbyist to innovator, using digital design tools from Adobe Photoshop and Adobe's creative suite to 3D immersive TiltBrush and online collaborative 3D immersive MasterpieceVR. Creatives collaborate globally – working with others to create, play and work. User creative forums and software platforms, online sandboxes for designers and coders – generate 3D virtual worlds and media platforms for interactive and unique story telling forms, and the design and build of products and engineering infrastructure.

Opportunities afforded by Creative Commons, open source, and a free share and exchange culture scaffold collective creative industries to generate innovation. Moreover, online collectors of quirky images, sounds and movies (pets, mishaps, slapstick humour), or even letter shapes discovered in random environments, re-invent the Surrealists' ready-mades to an internet media saturated generation. Some collectors trace trees of genealogy, history or antiques hoping to identify 'who they are' or 'what it is' by uncovering past journeys and migrations. Other collectors, collect virtual characters that are linked to geo-locators, e.g. PokemonGo.

Identities of creator-collaborator-collector are re-imagined. The notion of online identity can be multi-selves, avatar-selves, collaborative-selves. For some within the traditional corporate environment, 'time' is still the sought-after currency, whilst for the online media enabled generation, creative, collaborative, value-driven 'experience' is the new currency of desire. Desire for unique identity drives our choice of online activities. Is your online identity that of a creative, collaborator or collector, and how do you protect its value?

Vulnerable adults

Adults in assisted social housing or care homes expect IT access to communicate to their wider families. Councils, police and charities reported to CyberCare (April 2018) serious cyber abuse incidents occurring within these relationships and communities. Programmes for cyber awareness, early intervention, crisis clinics and champion programmes for these communities of adults and carers are crucial. These users include adults with learning difficulties, mental health challenges, adults across the autistic spectrum, adults caught in the recurring toxic trio of mental disorder, addiction and crime, and their service providers and carers.

Children, schools and youth

Schools and youth communities report a high incidence of cyber-bullying. A psychotherapist counsellor at a London School reported to the author that from her observations at least three quarters of all children in all year groups were involved with some forms cyber bullying incidents, some linked to incidents of sexual abuse.[51] The children's charity NSPCC reports that most children are affected by bullying. Their measures to combat Cyber Abuse involve using online games, stimulating conversations and controlling access through parental controls enabling the children and families to conquer the web by changing culture, education and technology.[52]

Trackers, perpetrators and criminals

The motivation behind this type of coercive and controlling unethical behaviour is usually driven by anger, hate, jealousies and/or unrealistic expectations of adult romantic or business relationships. Tracking may be used in conjunction with the misuse of media for sexual gratification where there is no face to face relationship or consent. The internet, including the

---

51. Conversation with child psychotherapist and counsellor at Institute of Group Analysis, IGA, NW3, London. 17th February 2018, At the Workshop. 'Sexual abuse: a perversion of attachment? (Part III)' Speakers: Arturo Ezquerro, Simon Partridge and Felicity de Zulueta, Chair: Mark Linington, Chair of Bowlby Centre's Executive Committee. This event is part of the Bowlby Centre's Clinical Forum programme, in association with the Institute of Group Analysis and the International Attachment Network.
52. https://www.nspcc.org.uk/preventing-abuse/keeping-children-safe/online-safety/

Dark Net, may be used for: the misuse of media data without consent with the sole aim of abuse, revenge, within dysfunctional relationships; the misuse of content to create violence and disruption for reasons of evil, terror and/or mental disorder; the illegal sale of harmful items or digital content for illegal commercial gain or terrorist activity. Often a cyber abuse tracker will be successfully convicted when their cyber abuse and hate crime is linked to or part of another criminal activity. Tracking and monitoring is linked to most cases of domestic homicide by a known perpetrator. There are challenges to securing evidence-based digital proof of the identity of perpetrators of cyber abuse.

Digital Identities as breached and fractured

Our online multi-selves and identities are formed through our share and exchange of products, services and communities within a global context. How do we protect these identities, minimise fraud, stolen identities and online hidden criminal activities? Professional bodies are taking on board the crucial need to create an online ethics supported by global legal framework. February 2018 saw the launch of the Global Centre for Cybersecurity (GCC) platform for cybersecurity coordination on a global scale, bringing together governments, business and law enforcement agencies. [53] At the World Economic Forum at Davos, January 2018, the Digital Identity Report indicates the need for digital identities to be connected, traceable and transparent enabled by a sustainable system, that facilitates inclusion, design and governance. The report states that "identity fraud is an indication that digital identities breaches can have a significant impact on our physical lives. Consumers need to be educated and trained to

53. http://theconversation.com/digital-dark-age-fears-stoked-by-davos-elite-do-little-to-address-cybersecurity-90874

understand that actions in the digital world have direct impact in the physical world, as our digital identity is primarily a representation of 'who we are' physically. "[54] Their understanding is that the notion of digital identity today is dangerous and at risk, moreover our digital identities are perceived as fractious and its landscape fractured.

54/ http://www3.weforum.org/docs/White_Paper_Digital_Identity_Threshold_Digital_Identity_Revolution_report_2018.pdf

2.5

CYBER ABUSE: SCENARIOS & STORIES

In our investigation of individuals who had reported cyber hacks, we found clear evidence that someone is or was hacking into their systems. The challenge is identifying who and why? How you might spot a hack?

Often the user observations point to unusual incidents on their IT systems or devices: e.g. laptops and phones. Observations include: calls being dropped or blocked, pop-ups produced by malware, proxy websites with different look and feel, on phones – noises, echoes, muffled sound during calls, IT systems and devices with slower processing speeds or with low battery life, some apps disappearing, new apps appearing, or proxy icons that hide covert spyware.

Often in the cases of targeted malicious abuse, the perpetrator will boast online to the victim's face or to friends and family that he has attacked the victim's system and is collecting so-called compromising information to humiliate her or gain custody of the children or ruin her business and reputation or uses this information to stalk and harass her. This may be a manifestation of personality disorder and/or controlling and coercive behaviour. As previously indicated the majority of perpetrators are males in a heteronormative relationship but this is not exclusively the case. In 4% of our cases the victims have been male in non-normative relationships. Statistical studies indicate that victim gender is 10-20% male: 80-90% female. Two women are killed each week by a current or former partner in England and Wales.[55] The six-month study by the University of Gloucestershire found stalking was present in 94% of the 358 cases of criminal homicides where there was a known perpetrator.[56] To clarify, not all stalking leads to murder but in 94% of these types of homicides – stalking and monitoring was present.

Data from hate crime and hate content understood to be the outcome of violence towards women and girls is collated by several charities, and government advocacy groups. These charities and advocacy groups in collaboration with research organisations, collect data, develop awareness, early and crisis intervention methods to combat this type of crime. They work with perpetrators, victims, their families and the wider community.[57]

In the CyberCare clinic population 2016/2017, one in four of people seeking support for domestic abuse, were being cyber abused, harassed, monitored or tracked via internet enabled apps or devices. [58]

55. https://www.refuge.org.uk/our-work/forms-of-violence-and-abuse/domestic-violence/domestic-violence-the-facts/

56. "The sample was drawn mainly from the Counting Dead Women website maintained by Karen Ingala Smith (2017). This website tracks the deaths of women that occur in the UK as a result of male violence in particular.

The website captures the majority of, but not all, deaths that occur. We first included all cases published on the site in our identified time frames of 2012, 2013 and 2014, and then excluded cases where the victim was not specifically targeted. By this we mean that we excluded cases of mistaken identity, those which occurred outside the UK where circumstances could not be verified, and those committed in the course of another crime like burglary or robbery. 40 cases were therefore discarded.

All remaining cases could be identified as having a targeted victim. We included cases of Honour Based Violence and sexual homicides, and also trawled media reports and Domestic Homicide Review (DHR) reports for any deaths not captured on the website. We identified 358 cases in all.'"

57. APPG led by MP Jess Phillips; Solace http://solacewomensaid.org/about-us/research-policy-recommendations/; Women's Aid; Violence Against Women and Girls VAWG; Refuge; Suzy Lamplugh Trust

58. Local Council One Stop Shop for Domestic Abuse - Cybercare clinic data 2016/2017, Cybercare.org.uk

How cyber abuse can affect the lives of individual victims?

At CyberCare we have clustered different types of suspects/perpetrators who carry out cyber abuse into a range of scenarios, or human stories. Often the police report that the perpetrators are found to be repeat offenders who target victims whom they perceive as vulnerable. Often there are aspects of social engineering where humans are manipulated in opening or unlocking access doors to their IT systems unwittingly. Often trusted marriages, relationships or friendships become dysfunctional, go sour and the suspect has become embittered with rage, hatred or jealous and turns on his loved one using cyber violence as his weapon.

Gendered pronouns are used here because heterosexual pairings where the man is the suspected or alleged perpetrator and the woman is the victim are over 90% of the reported cases, however there are cases of cyber violence where the suspected or alleged perpetrator is the woman. All human intimate relationships can be open to cyber abuse and cyber violence, be it, non-gendered, trans, gay or polyamorous, 4% of our use cases were male victims.[59]

Often the suspected or alleged perpetuator exhibits a likely mental disorder, be it borderline personality affective disorder or similar. Legal professionals working in Family Law have been heard to describe this behaviour as 'mad, bad and sad'. The suspected or alleged perpetrator needs to control and manipulate the victim with disregard for the victim's feelings and right to free will. Perhaps mental ill health and/or traumatic early childhood experiences have badly affected the suspected or

---

59. Cybercare use cases - June 2016 - March 2018. 4% of all victims were male.

alleged perpetrator's capacity to build, develop, negotiate, trusted and empathetic intimate relationships.

Often in family scenarios, children are used unwittingly or consciously as the go-between, transmitting the hacking method, be it virus, trojan or human engineering. Families in the process of divorce and separation often use their children as pawns in some sort of dysfunctional competitive game. Feelings of loyalty for one parent rather than the other can create damage to the psychological health of the children. In the context of a familial cyber battle, feelings of split loyalties might push the child to unwittingly endanger the parent who is being victimised. Sometimes the children themselves need to be safe-guarded from violent, physical, social, coercive or sexually inappropriate behaviour of the parent who is the alleged perpetrator. Sometimes both parents or members of the wider family can take on the role of perpetrators or support the Parent Perpetrator. Inappropriate and even cruel behaviour can be played out where separating parents both wage a cyber battle. Sometimes even in simple separation scenarios inconsistent parenting is evident in the sending of conflicting text messages to children from the different warring parents.

Human Scenarios – Real Stories

Our work in CyberCare requires both an understanding of IT systems and how they can be hacked into and how the information held there can be compromised, and how people use their IT systems, their smart phones and smart devices such as Smart TV, Games Consoles and household products which are internet enabled, commonly referred to as the Internet of Things - IOT. The most common hacks for organisations are enabled by mis-configuration and intruder threat. This is the same for the individual, families and communities, but here the control is not in the hands of the IT support and service department, guidelines from employers and employee behaviour. Here the individual needs to manage carefully their IT system, their IT lifestyle and retain legal and financial control of their own IT system. We have clustered these anonymised scenarios by perpetrator identities and intent, by victim's IT knowledge and capacities and by type of IT hack or IT vulnerability. Victims are referred through multiple channels, social and housing services at local councils, police, self-referrals, and cybersecurity business partner referrals. Here are anonymised descriptions of typical scenarios:

Unknown perpetrator: A man with feelings of fear, anxiety and paranoia, seeking support from social and health services. Remote access or spyware is found on across the IT system and on all devices. Open networks have been used to access the internet with the perpetrator unknown or not reported. Sometimes later reports suggest a perpetrator is attempting exploitation. It is probable that access to online identity was gained through online dating activities or previous business partners.

The tracker: A woman with children, in a failing domestic relationship with abusive husband. She seeks support from a domestic abuse charity. Spyware with default geo-locators found on her phone or the perpetrator is found to be accessing her iCloud.

The coercive controller: A woman with children, separated from her controlling and abusive husband. Divorce in process. Restraining order in place. Father plays computer games with children outside her home, using her Wi-Fi internet. After the Wi-Fi is secured he then accesses her new home IT system through a second iCloud. Children are told by the perpetrator to reset passwords across the IT system. The children become 'intruder threat' and give him access to her new IT system in her new home. Meanwhile he is threatening to kidnap children.

The business bully: A woman with a home business, worked with a boyfriend to set up her website. Later the relationship went sour. Ex- boyfriend is now threatening the reputation of the business by revenge web posting as he has sole control of her business website.

A victim in flight: A woman has escaped a failed relationship with abusive partner, now re-located in a safe house, with new devices, email and social media, logs onto her old email or social media account which offers geo-locators as a default feature, and thus in error alerts the perpetrator to her new location. Sometimes the victim has a public profile, sometimes the victim operates her lifestyle through many social media channels.

'Honour' motivated abuse: A young woman is seeking safety from her family who wish her to go abroad to marry a bridegroom against her will. They are searching for her. Charity social workers are seeking to protect her. She has geo-locators and spyware on her only phone, which is her only means of communication with the charity social workers.

Human slavery coercion: Human slavery victim is given orders using a mobile phone, but they have no other belongings with them. The phone is tracking and monitoring their movements; listening and viewing their actions and who they might talk to. The phone has spyware, geo-locators, cameras and audio capture. They are being continually threatened to take orders from their captors.[60]

APT – advanced persistent threat: A woman, maybe a mother, maybe with a business or profession. Years after divorce settlement, the ex-husband perpetrator might be perceived to be motivated by legal disputes over money and children but in fact is determined by his narcissistic or borderline personality disorder. This perpetrator is still tracking the woman on all her IT devices and systems, persistently targeting her over several years, over different countries and across different locations. Often accompanied by threatening online abuse through email and social media, and sometimes accompanied by continual legal disputes. In some cases, the perpetrator who has been imprisoned is now due for release. In some cases, the victim has not agreed to be a witness, so the Crown Prosecution Service CPS was not able to take the perpetrator to court. In some cases, the perpetrator has accused the victim in their community or and via the legal system to intimidate and threaten her and blackmail her into silence. In some cases, physical tracking by the perpetrator or paid proxies is observed. Across our use cases, APT cases are 8% of all referrals.

Who are the victims?

Some victims' profiles may point to factors of specific vulnerability; however, many have stories have developed which show their remarkable resilience. For some, specific vulnerabilities may be 'learned helplessness', language and cultural challenges; lack of basic

---

60. http://www.a21.org

IT knowledge and education to protect themselves by understanding logical systems. Often the victims have been under such duress due to persistent emotional, coercive and sometimes physical abuse they feel as if they have no residue of control or agency. Sometimes women are victims of a socio-economic reality where they are not wage earners because they are mothers or are in a traditional culture which has fostered their sense of dependency on patriarchal structures. Occasionally they are so traumatised and numb that they are fighting to find some memory of emotional and psychological resilience to fend off their aggressive and persistent perpetrator. Victims come from all walks of life, educational levels and socio-economic backgrounds. We aim to empower them to work with us to develop complex problem-solving skills to protect their IT system which may have been under attack across many levels. As the victims develop these skills – they become victim-survivors. We encourage them to develop their IT expertise and when able, to reach out to support others.

2.6

PRACTICAL SOLUTIONS TO TACKLE CYBER ABUSE

At CyberCare, our first priority is to protect victims from the threat of cyber abuse and the crime of coercion and violence and sometimes homicide; secondly is the capture of evidence to support perpetrator convictions and collect data patterns to support evidence-based policing and legal enforcement. Our approach is in line with the need to change cyber culture, cyber education, and technical cyber security. CyberCare provides victims with face to face support through our helpline, pop-up clinics and clinics at charities, services and councils, IT lifestyle clinics and support groups. We provide learning resources, technical support and recommended products. CyberCare provides training on different levels of education for service providers and end-user communities.

Collection of evidence may include: photos with embedded metadata, giving details of time, date and location. Circumstantial evidence, where an alleged perpetuator attempts to access the victim's cloud, such as social media or email (IP addresses that access the victim's network with logged time, location, date). However, IP addresses can be altered and hidden and do not necessarily prove the sender was sending the hack. Evidence is most effective when it is linked to physical evidence of incidents, or bullying, fraud and blackmail. Cyber incidents can corroborate and add additional evidence to other crime incidents and physical evidence. False personas, pseudo ID credentials and alternate digital identities are easily created leading to false trails.

Practical solutions require protective defence and need comprehensive systematic knowledge of IT systems. Using a logical, consistent risk assessment, vulnerabilities can be diagnosed. A problem-solving approach is necessary to unpick the technical complexity. Firstly, the victim needs to clearly identify the concerns. Log their observations and likely incidents of attack in order for the risks and vulnerabilities to be identified and prioritised across levels of the IT system. Visual examination of the devices and IT system can offer indications of potential vulnerabilities, spyware and hacking attacks. Invasive penetration testing can reveal and evidence the attack but not necessarily the identity of the attacker.

In addition, empathy and psychological skills can enable the victim-survivor to manage the dysfunctional emotional relationship with her known alleged perpetrator. Often within the broken or failing relationship, there are accelerating levels of anxiety, depression, trauma, anger, disappointed expectations and dashed hopes. The alleged perpetrator's anger may need to be managed skillfully to avoid escalation and the threat of violence against the victim-survivor and family. Support charities such as Rise Mutual, may offer perpetrator and family programmes to work through these unsettled feelings and traumatised emotional life.[61]

---

61. http://risemutual.org

Support charities (Solace, local councils' social housing teams, Women's Aid, Refuge, JWA, AWRC, IKWRO) offer the victim-survivor and families support, refuge and counselling.[62] CyberCare seeks to work to protect victim-survivors and their families in collaboration with social service providers, police and charities in this multi-agency context.

---

62. http://solacewomensaid.org, https://www.womensaid.org.uk, https://www.refuge.org.uk, http://www.jwa.org.uk, http://ikwro.org.uk, http://www.asianwomencentre.org.uk, http://risemutual.org

PART 3

RISKS OF THE DIGITAL AGE

by

Nick Ioannou
Founder of Boolean Logical Ltd

3.1

DATA COLLECTION

The incredible growth of the internet

The incredible growth of the internet over the past 20 years has seen a gigantic leap in how we communicate, consume information and interact with each other. Old boundaries of countries are pretty meaningless in our digital lives and the devices we use have shrunk to the point where we can have them with us 24/7. In the 80s you could count the number of TV channels on one hand. You had to buy a newspaper if you wanted to read it and doing any form of research meant visiting the library. Compare that to now, where we all can freely communicate with each other and source our information not just from official media channels and trusted sources, but from social media platforms, companies, pretty much anyone and anywhere. But the truth is, it is not free, we must give the gatekeepers personal information about ourselves to access many of these systems, information that if it falls into the hands of criminals can be used for identity fraud, theft and extortion.

Currently there are over 60 social media / social

networking and messaging systems; some are more popular in certain countries like China, while others are actually owned by mainstream social media giants. For instance, Facebook also owns WhatsApp and Instagram, Microsoft owns LinkedIn, and Google owns YouTube. And because of this, data can be shared between the parent company and the social media platform they bought, which in many cases was the whole point of buying them for the data in their customer user profiles.

Personal data

We think nothing of giving up our title, name, address, date of birth, gender, mobile number and email address in order to use an online service, and quickly scroll to the end of the terms and conditions acceptance page, without reading any of it, to click Accept. It's not as if reading it will really make any difference! You cannot say 'I agree to this bit, but not that bit'; it's an all or nothing choice, and you have probably decided to use the service because everyone else you need to communicate with is already using it. Laid out in those long terms and conditions it clearly states what information they will collect, and the fact that they may use it to sell targeted adverts and build a detailed profile of you. In effect you are paying for the 'free' basic service with your personal data.

When George Orwell wrote 1984, he never envisioned us carrying the telescreens in our pockets, complete with location tagging as well. We post pictures of ourselves, our children, our friends and family, especially pets, and even our food, and each picture may include geo tagging location information as well as the date and time the picture was taken. We also give information on our schools and education, our hobbies and pastimes, our cars, where and what we are doing and who with. Every like, every message, every advert clicked, every purchase within the platform, it all goes into building a profile of you. However, that is not all. If I give you half the pieces of a jigsaw puzzle, while you cannot finish it, you can definitely have a good idea of what the image is about after spending a couple of hours trying to solve it. The same applies to your profile, there are enough pieces of the puzzle to allow these companies to fill in a lot of the gaps and make some good guesses about the rest.

Of course, the trick is we don't really realise just how much information we are giving away, because it happens over time in subtle ways, like when we post something innocently like a 'thanks mum you're the best' on social media. Nothing wrong with that is there, except you may have just helped a criminal work out your mother's maiden name. You see, cyber criminals love social media, because it takes all the guesswork out of who to target and gives them hooks to easily create believable emails and messages based on the information we have posted. It's quite easy to fake an email; all you need is a genuine copy of the email from a particular company or service and you have everything you need to replicate it. Even if you don't have a genuine email to start with, there is enough imagery and text on nearly every major company's website to build a convincing fake. However, if that fake email is asking you to update your credit card details or security questions, or open an attachment for a refund, you could unwittingly become a cybercrime statistic.

The thing is that cybercrime is now part of organised crime. It is massively profitable, heavily resourced, with little chance of getting caught as most of the crimes are committed by criminals in other countries. The skill levels required to be involved in cybercrime has also plummeted as criminals sell online services to other criminals. Plus, there are the huge database breaches/hacks that gave the criminals a massive head start from the Yahoo breach in 2013, Uber in 2016 and Equifax in 2017. Regularly updating your passwords is the best way to reduce the value of these hacks, but this means really changing your passwords, not just adding a 1 at the end. The fact is, it's not just emails and passwords the criminals have, they may also have your mobile number. If you receive text message updates from your bank, save the number and call it something you recognise. That way if you receive a fake bank message, you'll be suspicious immediately.

Useful online advice

But not all data hacks are due to criminals. The data analytics firm Cambridge Analytica, which has been accused of harvesting millions of Facebook profiles without permission, did so apparently via a personality app called "thisisyourdigitallife" that utilized a developer feature called Facebook Login, so people wouldn't have to create a username and password to sign in, but use their Facebook account instead. And when they agreed to use Facebook Login, they also agreed to give access to their Facebook profile and friends list. So not only did the people give extra information about themselves as part of the personality test, they also handed over a lot more information than they expected to. A similar trick is the online survey, often for a voucher or prize draw, and may contain brand logos despite having no connection whatsoever to those brands. Just because it says you'll receive a £100 worth of Tesco vouchers, it doesn't mean it's genuine, or will arrive in the form of a £10 off voucher when you spend £100 and just give you 10 vouchers. So please be wary of online surveys, quizzes and personality tests, firstly for the questions they may ask and also for the additional access to your social media information that may be requested 'for your convenience.'

When you are doing any online shopping, if you get asked to save your payment card details, as convenient as it is, please say no. This way if someone else gets access to your account credentials or computer, you haven't given them everything they need. If you can, either use a credit card or PayPal rather than a debit card, as both give additional protection for goods and services ordered over £100. Online retailers get hacked just like any other company; so if the worst did happen, money isn't being taken straight out of your bank account, unlike a debit card. You can also turn on extra password security on a credit card or two-step verification on PayPal where you get sent a code via a text message to your mobile.

To prevent identify fraud, never enter your passport number or driving licence as part of a security question, the only time you are asked for these is if you are adding advanced passenger information for a flight on an airline's website or hiring a car. If these appear as part of a drop-down list of security or recovery options on any other website, you are probably on a fake website that is phishing you for sensitive personal information. Genuine recovery security questions are things like a memorable place or your favourite actor, nothing that could be used for ID theft.

Privacy settings

I live by the maxim that there is no guaranteed privacy with anything you share online. Anything you post into social media may be seen by people you'd rather were not able to and, while you can rely on security settings to dictate with whom you share the information initially, after that it can be shared again, copied, photographed or stolen. If you don't want to risk anything you write or share, don't put it online, it's that simple. Unfortunately, life isn't that simple, and deleting social media accounts is a step too far for most of us. So please ask yourself whether anything you post online could be used against you or would be helpful to a criminal. Updating your social media profile to say to the whole world you are at the airport for a two-week holiday may not be the best idea. So, the first thing to do is see what information the social media companies you use have on you, then limit who has access to your profiles via the privacy options to just your friends and family.

For Facebook this can be found at:
www.facebook.com/privacy
while information on what Facebook collects about you can be found at: www.facebook.com/about/privacy/

For LinkedIn go to: /www.linkedin.com/psettings/
and www.linkedin.com/help/linkedin/answer/50191/accessing-your-account-data

The amount of data Google has on you can be vast, so for ease they split everything into 32 products to make downloading your data more manageable, and created a dedicated website at https://takeout.google.com/

Other social media services will have similar features to let you decide on your privacy settings and how to download your data. The main thing is to be aware of what you have given them and decide if you are happy with that. You actually have a lot more control over your data now then you ever did, backed by new laws that are now in force.

3.2

DATA PROTECTION AND THE LEGISLATION

GDPR – General Data Protection Regulation

If you live in Europe and are active online, you will probably have received lots of emails mentioning GDPR, asking for consent to stay in contact and talking about a new law that is effective from the 25th May 2018. GDPR stands for General Data Protection Regulation, which replaces the older Data Protection Act of 1998 in the UK. As you know, a lot has changed in 20 years; in fact most of the current social media giants haven't been around that long. One of the oldest is LinkedIn, which started in 2002, Facebook didn't start until 2005, with Twitter a year later in 2006. Instagram and Pinterest both started in 2010 and Snapchat and Google+ in 2011. Remember, back in 1998, there was no ADSL broadband; home users generally had dial up internet access only and sharing video or photos taken on a mobile was impossible as no phones had a camera back then. Since then, various companies have been collecting data on us for years, hoping to find a use for it in time and monetise it, often without our knowledge.

It's clear, a revision and rethink when it comes to data protection laws has been long overdue.

So, after years of debate in the EU, the new General Data Protection Regulation (I'll refer to it as GDPR from now on) was agreed to get everyone on the same level across the EU, as different EU countries had quite varied data protection laws. But GDPR is also enforced to protect the personal data of all EU citizens from companies and organisations worldwide, not just in the EU. Now before anyone mentions Brexit, GDPR will become an equivalent UK law, so don't think this is something that is going to change any time soon. Also, and this is a big one, it applies to both 'analog' and 'digital' data, so anything written down, printed, emailed or stored digitally that contains personal data is covered by this law. As to what constitutes personal data, the legislation defines this as pretty much anything that can be used to identify someone, directly or indirectly. In practical terms this becomes an extensive ever-growing list, covering a lot more than what immediately comes to mind like your name, address, email, telephone number, bank account, etc, to include social, economic, cultural, physical, mental and genetic factors. GDPR also talks about 'processing' which is a rather vague term that just about means doing absolutely anything with the data, including but not limited to, storing it, sharing it, altering it, or deleting it.

The six principles of GDPR

Now let's actually look at what GDPR means to you so you don't need to read all the 57,500+ words of the new legislation, starting with the six overall principles of the act which sets out the main responsibilities for organisations.

Firstly, that personal data is processed lawfully, fairly and in a transparent manner in relation to individuals. The important bit here is the transparent manner, so they have to be open and tell you what they are collecting and why, in a way that you can understand, rather than hidden away in small print with lots of legal language.

The second principle is that personal data is collected for specified, explicit and legitimate purposes and not further processed in a manner that is incompatible with those purposes. So here, the reason why they asked for the personal data, cannot be changed and be used for something else that has nothing to do with the reason you gave them the information in the first place. So, if you were asked for your date of birth in order to be sent birthday discount offers, they couldn't then use it to send you life assurance quotes or medical insurance.

The third principle is that personal data is adequate, relevant and limited to what is necessary in relation to the purposes for which they are processed. This principle is to make sure you are only asked to give information that is relevant and in context of the service provided. Too many organisations in the past have asked for things that are not required in order to build a customer profile of you. A date of birth is not required for any online shopping, unless it is for age restricted goods; in the same way it is not generally required if you walk into a shop to buy something. The same applies to your marital status, dependants and household income, you wouldn't tell this to a shop cashier.

Okay, so far nothing to worry about; all good.

The fourth principle is quite a biggie: that personal data is accurate and, where necessary, kept up to date;

every reasonable step must be taken to ensure that personal data that is inaccurate, having regard to the purposes for which it is processed, is erased or rectified without delay. Here it squarely puts the onus on the organisation to make sure what they have is accurate, and if you tell them to correct something or that they don't need it anymore, it is corrected or erased.

The fifth principle states that personal data must be kept in a form which permits identification of data subjects for no longer than is necessary for the purposes for which the personal data are processed. So basically, once a company has no reason to keep data on you, they need to remove it from their systems.

Lastly, the sixth principle is all about security, that your data is processed in a manner that ensures appropriate security of the personal data, including protection against unauthorised or unlawful processing and against accidental loss, destruction or damage. This ensures that safeguards are in place, which you would expect anyway; though, if the past decade has taught us anything about data security, it is that there is no such thing as 100% security.

So, in order to meet the requirements of the principles, organisations need to know and document the Who, What, Why, Where and When regarding your personal information. There are more, they just don't begin with a W, like How, Access, Security and others. Now you would expect most organisations to know this, but the truth is that your data is probably in more places than they realise; so GDPR makes them evaluate what they have, why they have it, who it is on, when they received the information, where they put it, how they intend to use it and with whom they will be sharing it with. And that is no small task; so don't expect small businesses and organisations to be up to the same speed as major corporations who have been spending over a year preparing.

The Legislation

The legislation says that for organisations to process any personal information they must first have a lawful basis for processing the information. This isn't the same as the first principle to process information lawfully, fairly and in a transparent manner. This is the actual reason and justification for requesting and storing the information in the first place.

GDPR allows for six different reasons:

1. Consent
2. Contract
3. Legal obligation
4. Vital interests
5. Public task
6. Legitimate interests

The one most people will be interested in is *Consent*, where you have agreed to give your personal info, but now the legislation gives you a lot more control than previously. Now consent must be freely given, specific, with an active opt-in (i.e. you had to click yes – it wasn't a pre-ticked or opt-out box in case you missed it) as well as being clear and concise as to what you are agreeing to. There has been a lot of misunderstanding though about consent, with organisations emailing all their customers asking to renew their consent to process their data, otherwise they won't receive any more communication from them, despite those customers having paid annual subscriptions or recently placed orders. One of the main factors of consent is that organisations need to allow you to easily withdraw your consent at any time – it's your data not theirs after all – but there may be contractual considerations to take into account on both sides. Also, there are additional rules around children, who have to be aged 13 or over to be able to give consent for an online service aimed at their age group.

For more sensitive data, which GDPR calls 'special category' data, the six lawful basis reasons are not enough, and one of ten conditions must also be met.

Special category data is basically the following:

1. Race
2. Ethnic origin
3. Health information
4. Biometrics
5. Genetic data
6. Trade union membership
7. Political opinions
8. Religious beliefs
9. Sex life or
10. Sexual orientation

Organisations are expected to implement extra safe-guards for special category data, as this can be used for bias and hate crimes as well as extortion or fraud if it falls into the hands of criminals. Further details on this can be found on https://ico.org.uk/for-organisations/guide-to-the-general-data-protection-regulation-gdpr/lawful-basis-for-processing/special-category-data/

Rights

As mentioned previously, to protect and manage your personal data, GDPR has been put into place and the legislation provides the following eight rights for individuals:

1. The right to be informed
2. The right of access
3. The right to rectification
4. The right to erasure
5. The right to restrict processing
6. The right to data portability
7. The right to object
8. Rights in relation to automated decision making and profiling

The right to be informed means a lot more than you think, as organisations must now tell you their reasons for collecting your personal data, how long they will keep it for, who they will share it with, contact information, your rights and more. This needs to be done when they collect your data; so expect to see a web link to a privacy notice, which will then take you to a few paragraphs of text and maybe a tick box to confirm you understand it.

The second right individuals have is the right of access to their personal data. As an EU citizen, you can request what is known as a 'data subject access request' to an organisation either verbally or in writing (emails and social media messages count) which is basically just asking them officially 'please can I have a copy of any personal information you have on me'. This also includes things like attendance to events or courses, rather than just information you gave them. Organisations have the right to ask you to prove who you are, or, if the request is via a third party, evidence that they are entitled to act on your behalf. Typically, they have up to 30 days to respond and in most cases, they are not allowed to charge you anything to reply. Over time, I expect many companies to create self-service web portals, so you can quickly and easily access your data and make any decisions based on your rights: like the third right, the right to rectification, to correct any inaccurate personal data or to complete missing information.

Next, you have the right to erasure, more commonly known as the right to be forgotten. Now there are a lot of scenarios where the right to erasure does not apply, otherwise you could ask to be forgotten after receiving a parking ticket. GDPR does not override other laws, so if you have had any form of contract with an organisation, they are obliged to keep records. If an organisation has shared your data with others or made it publicly accessible, each recipient must also be contacted by the organisation regarding the erasure, unless this proves to be a mammoth undertaking. Slightly less drastic than erasure is the right to temporarily restrict processing, which permits an organisation to store the personal data, but not use it. This right could be used when you are contesting the accuracy of the information or do not want it erased by the organisation because you are in dispute with them or someone else and require the data. This is not the same as the right to object to the processing of your personal data. For direct marketing purposes, the right to object is absolute and cannot be denied. Also, the right to object is not the same as erasure, if you ask an organisation to remove you from a marketing mailing list and not to contact you again, they cannot delete you completely, as they wouldn't know not to contact you in the future.

The right to data portability is there to basically allow you to obtain and transfer your data from one service to another, without incurring extra charges. This is quite an ambitious requirement as every service is different; so, in order to make it workable, it is limited to the data you have given them yourself, whether typed or uploaded like photos or videos. It does not cover data that was derived or inferred by the organisation about you as a result of being a customer or user. Lastly, there are provisions on automated decision-making and profiling of an individual, where decisions are made without any human involvement; you can request human intervention or challenge a decision. Think of the 'computer says no' sketch from the show Little Britain.

So, what happens if an organisation messes up and loses your personal data, discloses it to unauthorised individuals, accidentally deletes it or it is hacked, commonly known as a data breach? Well, now there is a 72-hour breach notification limit for them to inform the appropriate supervisory authority, but this is based on them having become aware that they have lost personal data in the first place. In many cases months (even years) have gone by before an organisation is aware of what had happened, so the 72-hour limit may not make much of a difference overall, except it stops organisations trying to brush it under the carpet and hide the fact that it happened, once they know about it. Once they have informed the supervisory authority, they are then obliged to inform you of the nature of the breach, contact details of their Data Protection Officer, the likely consequences and mitigation measures they have taken or steps you can take. However, if the personal data they have lost is encrypted, they don't need to inform you, just the supervisory authority, about the incident. Just make sure any breach notifications you receive are genuine, as I expect that criminals will try to capitalise on them whenever there is a major database breach, in order to get you to either click on a malicious link or divulge credentials.

There is a lot more to GDPR, covering international transfers, contracts, penalties and much more, but we have covered the core of the regulation. If you are having trouble sleeping and need something to read, you can find out more about GDPR at the Information Commissioner's Office (ICO) at https://ico.org.uk

3.3

COUNTER SOCIAL ENGINEERING

For centuries we have been taught to trust and respect our banks, corporations and the authorities, which is required in a fair and just world. Except the world has changed incredibly quickly over the past 20 years. Old tried and tested ways of banking and finance, together with communication in general, have been replaced with digital solutions that require either a mobile phone or internet connection, often both. Many people are overwhelmed by this pace of change, especially if they were born in the last century, and criminals are exploiting this, together with our trusting nature, to bypass the security of these digital solutions through social engineering, getting us to willingly divulge confidential information or carry out actions which compromise us further.

But what is in it for the criminals?

Well it all comes back to fraud, theft, extortion and utilising your computing assets for their own purposes (like cryptocurrency mining). If the criminals can glean the right information from you, they can request a copy of your birth certificate and from that open bank accounts and take out loans, all in your name. Alternatively, your files could be held to ransom, your bank credentials and credit card details used fraudulently; the list goes on. What can I say; the criminals are quite creative in finding ways to monetise our information, but they have to get to it first.

As each digital solution has layers of security built-in, criminals need to find a way to bypass the security in order to succeed, and while they can use technology to hack these systems, it takes resources, time and advanced skills to do so. It is so much simpler and quicker for the criminals to trick us into handing over the keys without us realising. So how do we counter the criminals who are manipulating us for financial gain? In order to do this, we need to take a step back and look at all the ways they can communicate with us. They can email us, phone us or send us a message, either by SMS mobile text or via a social media platform. New words have been created to describe this based around the word 'fishing' as in fishing for information. Email based fraud is called 'phishing', while telephone-based voice scams are called 'vishing' and message-based scams or SMS phishing is called 'smishing'. The bit to remember though is that the criminals are not restricted to just one method and can use a combination of these to try and convince you of who they say they are.

Fake social media profiles are also a key component utilised by cyber criminals, though the social media companies are fighting back. In one report Facebook purged over 583 million fake accounts in the first three months of 2018. Because you do not need anything other than an email address to set up a social media profile, and you do not need any form of ID to setup an email address, you can see where I am going here.

So, the criminals create thousands of fake social media profiles, because it doesn't actually cost them anything; and a lot of people communicate over social media rather than email, so it helps build their illusions as thousands of 'people' cannot be wrong (except those thousands don't actually exist).

So, let's start with phishing.

According to the antivirus firm Sophos, 89% of phishing attacks are by organized crime. Just like fishing, you select a bait and go where you know there are lots of opportunities to catch fish; phishing is no different. The criminals choose services where they know there is a good chance of you being a customer or user, like TV licensing, high street banks, retailers like Amazon, email systems like Hotmail/Outlook.com and Gmail. com, even government departments like HM Revenue & Customs. Next, they offer the bait: 'there is an issue with your account', 'payment has failed', 'we have received a password reset request', 'you are due a refund', 'we have shipped your order'; whatever it is, it's generally a lie. I've even seen fake court summons and land registry charges; do not underestimate the creativeness of the criminals.

There will also be a hook: 'if you do not respond your account will be frozen', 'this is urgent', 'there is a very short time limit'. You get the idea, and the criminals are hoping you don't spot that the email address is not quite right, or the website address they are sending you to is slightly different to the real one. If you click on what they want you to click on, you are then taken to a login page or some type of security challenge for you to verify yourself. It is these credentials they are after and more, like your credit card and bank details.

You may then be taken to a 'thank you' page, because the criminals want you to be unaware of what has happened. That is, of course, if the criminal's intention wasn't just to get you to visit the website to try and infect your machine using automated scripts looking for vulnerabilities.

Sometimes the phishing attack is timed to coincide with an actual event like a major data breach or system upgrade; it's just sent out before the real one. These can be really hard to spot, because they are not unexpected. Not clicking on any links is still the best advice; always go manually to the website of the service or organisation via your web browser. The same applies to attachments, especially PDF attachments which may just contain a glorified link to take you to a fake landing page.

Telephone based voice scams or 'vishing'

Is particularly nasty as many of the victims are elderly. The fraudster calls out of the blue and claims to be from anywhere ranging from the police, the telecoms company, a marketing company doing a survey, even Microsoft (that one has been going on for over a decade) advising you that they have detected a virus on your computer. The lies being told will lead up to you telling the fraudster your credit card or bank details for a refund or a payment, as well as giving up other 'useful' information that could be used later on. Technology allows the fraudsters to use "call spoofing" to falsify the telephone number displayed and even ask you to call them back, but keep the line open, tricking you into thinking you've made a call.

If you do receive a call from anyone claiming to be your bank, a utility or service provider, you can challenge them to verify themselves, or better still ask them for their name and department only and hang up. Call someone you know or even a local taxi service; it doesn't matter, it's just to make sure the line is clear in case it is a fraudster and they are still on the line. Then look up the customer services number online of whoever called you and call them back. If the person is genuine, you will be able to get through to either them or someone in their team. Never give your PIN number for any bank or credit cards if asked, or any form of two factor information like a code from a PINsentry or banking app.

Message based scams or SMS phishing known as 'smishing'

Can be very effective as the smaller screen of a smartphone makes it harder to spot that the message itself is fake as well as the website the link takes you to. Smishing messages tend to be short and contain a look-a-like domain or a shortened hyperlink via services like Bit.ly in order to disguise the link. Bit. ly itself isn't malicious, it's just also being used by criminals. Legitimate messages from a bank, service provider or company wouldn't generally contain a Bit.ly shortened link. Phishing attacks can also be carried out over social media messaging systems like WhatsApp or Facebook Messenger, it just needs to be able to contain a hyperlink to a website to be effective.

Fake social media accounts

Criminals may convince you of a whole variety of things, ranging from fake surveys, bogus competitions,

even fake jobs. In general, beware of jobs that claim you are a financial adviser and require you to deposit money into your bank account, only for you to transfer it into another account minus a 10% fee. This is just money laundering disguised as a job. Online dating is also a good target for the criminals, with romance scams costing some people thousands. You can do what is known as a reverse image search of any profile pictures, which checks where else the image appears on the web. If it is fake it tends to appear in lots of places and you can see if it has been used in other social media profiles. Online dating fraudsters normally use an excuse as to why you cannot meet up or make video calls, like a military service tour due to finish, or they're spending three months helping rebuild a village in a third world country, so internet access is limited.

Helpdesk scam

The bogus helpdesk scam is another nasty fraud, where either they call you or you call them. Yes, I did say you could call them, because they pay to be high up in online search engine listings for the helpdesks of certain companies; so instead of calling the genuine company you end calling a scammer. Typically, the scenario they run you through is the same, where they ask you for your credentials and then to visit a website to establish remote access to your computer. They then show you something to prove there is a problem, but it's all fake. Next, they request payment to fix the problem or sell you a bogus subscription. Either way, it's bad news, because they have installed something on your computer, they have your credentials and your credit card details. If anyone calls you and tells you they have detected a problem or wants you to verify yourself in any way, ask them to put their request in writing (don't give an email address or postal address) and hang up the call.

Impersonation

Impersonating the boss is also a good way for fraud-sters to make a lot of money by asking for funds to be urgently paid to a new supplier to close a deal, timed when the real boss is hard to contact because they are about to get on a long-haul flight or attending a golfing charity day. Of course, the new supplier isn't real, though the bank account is. This is known as CEO fraud and in order for it to work the fraudsters do their research, unlike the scams sent out to thousands of people at the same time. They know the names of key people, maybe upcoming projects and have even already phished the email credentials of the boss. Fail-ing that, they can create a fake personal email address because most employees wouldn't know their bosses personal email address.

The way to avoid falling for most social engineering scams is first not to panic; anything to do with money and a sense of urgency needs to set off alarm bells. Trust your instincts, if something feels even slightly wrong, start to look for clues that will show you it is fake. Look at the email address, the tone, is it too impersonal or too formal. Ask yourself if you would expect to be contacted this way rather than a formal old-fashioned letter in the post. If there is a file attachment, question why, especially if it is a zip file, which can be used to hide the file from security systems. If there is a company mentioned that needs paying or to claim a refund, do not follow any links, instead manually visit their website. Hover over any links and see where it wants to take you, but if you accidently click on a link and it takes you to a website asking you to login, please, please do not login.

The rule is, if you cannot verify something or someone, assume it is fake or a lie until you can establish the truth, and then double check by contacting the relevant customer services department. Remember we are up against organized crime, it is big business, global and very profitable.

3.4

BANKING, APPS AND PASSWORDS

Our lives have become digital whether we like it or not, with everyday services from banking, to accessing local government services, having moved to a partial or completely digital online platform. We don't need to walk into a travel agent to book a flight or reserve a hotel room or visit the ticket desk to buy a train ticket. We can purchase a vast range of goods and services, including our groceries from our smartphones due to the ease of apps. But despite the ubiquitous nature of apps today with over 2 million different apps available, they have been around for less than 10 years. The first Apple iPhone only came out in 2007 and both the Apple App Store and Google Android Market (now called Google Play) didn't arrive until 2008. Apps were an instant success, small easy to use intuitive smartphone programs that did exactly what they said and little else. This was a world apart from traditional software and websites accessed via a desktop computer or laptop.

Banking was already ahead of the game, as we have had telephone banking since the 1980's and online banking via a website since 1999, so the addition of banking apps was a logical step. Not everything is done with an app though, and ecommerce allowed websites to be much more than information portals. Nearly every major high street retailer has an online presence and the utility companies have added online self-service account management for their customers. Each of the websites or apps, require an account to identify you and normally a password to protect unauthorised access; and in a short space of time we have gone from having to remember a few phone numbers, to having to remember dozens of passwords.

Every year we add more and more passwords as our digital lives expand into new areas of our lives, as well the constant pressure to update our passwords for various security reasons. The resulting effect is that most of us cannot cope with the sheer number of passwords we have, so reuse what we consider to be a good password in multiple places.

What is in a password?

Take a step back and ask yourself how many different online logins and passwords do you think you have? Here are 33 entries just off the top of my head, the true list is closer to 100 for myself.

Finance & Utilities	Online Shopping	Social Media	Online services	Travel
online banking	Amazon	LinkedIn	email	Congestion Charge
PayPal	Tesco	Facebook	Apple ID	Trainline
mobile network	John Lewis	Twitter	Microsoft ID	British Airways
electricity utility	Costco	Pinterest	Dropbox	Hotels.com
gas utility	Debenhams	Meetup		Marriott Hotels
water utility	Pizza company	Instagram		
council tax	Tastecard	Slack		
telephone network		Eventbrite		
Sky TV				

So, let's say for argument's sake, most people have around 50 online accounts that need a password. Unless you write them down somewhere and refer to it every time you need to login, you will stick to a limited number of passwords that you can remember. But what we consider to be a good strong password that is hard for someone else to guess, is not that strong for a computer to guess by literally trying every possible combination. You can test this out at https://howsecureismypassword.net/ which will quickly show you if a password can be broken instantly, as it is on a common passwords list. Just take the length of time estimates with a pinch of salt, as computing power is increasing at such a rapid exponential rate that what took years to compute a year ago, could soon take days. Adding numbers, capital letters and non-standard characters like a question mark or @ sign can help stop other people guessing your password if it is based on guessable things about you, but only makes it slightly harder for a computer to guess.

Also, the password for any given service may have to be changed. They may ask you to update it and change your password as a security precaution if they have noticed any unusual activity on their systems, or they have actually been compromised. Cyber criminals also know this; so send out their own bogus password update requests to trick you into handing over your login credentials and password. Best to ignore any password update requests by email or text message and just manually visit the website of the service concerned (never click on a link in a password update request) when you go to login, if the request is genuine you will normally be prompted to update your password.

So how do you choose a strong password that you can remember?

Firstly, let's change the word 'password' into 'passphrase' and string three or four words together. These can be a phrase like 'TooManyCooks' or a jumble of random words 'SteelJellyBrush' but to meet a lot of the password rules you need to add a number or two and possibly non-standard characters. Try to avoid though, numbers like your year of birth or anything that can be found in any of your social media profiles. So now you have a strong password for one service, only 49 more to go! The advice to not reuse passwords for different services and not write them down, while good advice, is somewhat unrealistic for most people. So, a compromise is needed, actually writing down your passwords (or hints to your passwords) on paper can still be more secure than having a folder in your email system called Passwords.

Just remember though...

If you keep everything in a small notebook or wallet, think about what happens if you lose it. If you can, just list the passwords and very limited login info or website details. Another compromise is to have a set or group of passwords for different things like money, shopping, email, utilities. Again though, remember that using the same password again and again is a really bad idea because if one of those systems is compromised and your credentials are leaked online, criminals now have automated software checking common online services to see if you have used the same email address and password.

A subscription to a password manager service can really make life a lot easier as they remember the individual passwords and all you have to remember is the one really strong password. Some like Dashlane, Lastpass and F-Secure KEY even have a free option, though if you want to use the service across multiple devices you'll need to upgrade. But the best password is one that is also protected with what is known as two factor authentication (2FA) or two step verification. After you enter your password you are then asked to enter a code which is typically sent to you in a text message to your mobile phone or from an app you have linked to your account. So, anyone trying to access your account, not only needs your password, but also access to your mobile phone. So even if your credentials are leaked online, you are still protected. The best part is that a lot of online services like email, Apple ID, Microsoft ID, social media, PayPal and Amazon, it is free to turn on this extra layer of security.

Two factor authentication

This is not a new process; the banks have been using it for years for online banking. You may have a device like a Barclays PINsentry card reader or a HSBC Secure Key at home, these are the second factor used when you need to authenticate yourself to the bank. These days though, the majority of online banking can now be done via the bank's own mobile app and digital versions of the two factor devices are now included in these apps, so you don't need to worry about carrying another device. Security is built into the banks smartphone apps from the start and they are linked to your device handset or mobile number, making it more secure than computer browser based online banking. Just make sure you only download them from an official app store or follow the link from the bank's website. Some of the banking apps also have a feature called 'personal greeting' which you can set to display something only you will expect to see, so that when you login you know are logging to the correct app. If the greeting is missing, you'll know that it is not the genuine login screen and being faked. Also, beware of third party banking apps and websites that claim to manage your bank accounts as these can be fake or potential routes to compromise you if they get hacked. Best to stick to your banks own apps and never follow a link from a text message or email, even if it is claiming to be from your own bank.

Lastly with regards to the two factor authentication via your banking apps or devices, if anyone calls you and claims to be from your bank and then asks you to verify yourself by giving them your two factor authentication code, hang up immediately The same goes for card details, passwords or PIN numbers, the criminals may already have a certain amount of information on you to try and convince you they are genuine; so please don't be fooled by them giving you the last 4 digits of your card number and asking you to verify the rest.

So, smartphone and tablet apps have become the norm for a large percentage of our personal computing activities in the space of a decade, and the cybercriminals know this. They try to get their malicious apps into the mainstream app stores, but this is proving to be much more difficult than the many unofficial ones around the world. That said Google removed over 700,000 Android apps in 2017, and while only a small percentage were outright malicious, that is still a lot of potential victims. If you suspect you may have fallen foul to a malicious smartphone app, please inform your bank immediately so they can monitor your accounts.

In-app purchases

There is also another way apps can drain your bank account, except that this time it is actually legal. I'm referring to 'In-app purchases' where you are charged for additional content, premium features or even virtual currency in a game. Many 'freemium' apps (apps that are initially free but have optional paid premium content) allow you to make multiple in-app purchases, with some popular games allowing you to spend up to £99.99 for in-game virtual currency as many times as you like. Because of the real danger of being able to spend a lot of money unwittingly in a short space of time, I encourage everyone to disable in-app purchases on their devices and require a password on every app purchase (free apps can be excluded).

You can always turn the ability to make in-app purchases back on anytime you like, but this way you cannot accidentally press something and find yourself instantly charged. Apps and passwords are not going to be replaced anytime soon, so we need to find secure solutions to managing our digital identities, because if we do not, the criminals will.

3.5

MINIMISE YOUR CYBER PROFILE

The sheer number of malicious programs (malware) now in circulation is a mind boggling 700 million according to the March 2018 McAfee Labs Threats Report and growing at rate over 250,000 per day. That is a lot of malicious programs to protect yourself from, but as the saying goes, they only need to be lucky once; you need to be lucky every time.

So how do you stay safe and minimise your cyber profile, or potential attack surface you present to the criminals? Let's break it down into six steps.

1. Reduce the overall number of known vulnerabilities on your computer and smartphone that could be exploited criminals, by regularly updating or patching your system and software. The criminals can move extremely quickly and create malware that exploits vulnerabilities for a fraction of the cost than in previous years, due to cloud computing, crime as a service software (yes criminals sell to other criminals) and automation. So as a result, every week there is a security software patch from a major software publisher trying to fight back and close the gaps

in security. So, while running updates and patching is annoying and time consuming, getting infected is much worse. If you have a computer that you only use occasionally, make a point of turning it on once a week, just to run updates. If you prefer to turn off computers at night, the updates may not happen automatically, so when you are finished and about to power off, check for updates in your system and main software packages that you use first.

2. Next, after making sure everything is up to date, you need good antivirus software. Do not be fooled into thinking you do not need antivirus for a mac, and, yes, modern PCs have antivirus built-in; it's just very basic. It is not just traditional computers that need antivirus as Android mobiles also can benefit; however, you don't need to worry about antivirus on an Apple iPhone as there isn't any available even if you wanted it. Free antivirus will give you a certain amount of protection, but considering what is at stake, it is a small investment to purchase premium antivirus, especially as multiple machine licences or 3-year licences are now available for only slightly more money. So, the question is which one do you choose? Any of the award winning mainstream offerings are good, like Bitdefender, Kaspersky or Malwarebytes, as well as newer offerings like Heimdal PRO. At any given point, one will be rated higher than the others by somebody; so the fact you have premium antivirus protection is the important bit. Just remember to shop around rather than accept the auto-renewal price.

3. How you connect to the internet is the next area to look at. Here two technologies can

keep you safe: a Domain Name Server (DNS) filtering service and a Virtual Private Network (VPN) service. Every website address you type into a web browser needs to be looked up and translated into a numerical internet protocol (IP) address. This is normally provided by your internet service provider, but you can use third party services like Quad9.net or OpenDNS.com which provide additional security by blocking websites that they know to be malicious before you even get there. Both services do not require any software or hardware; just a tweak on your network settings. Quad9 is completely free too for both businesses and individuals, while OpenDNS has a free personal tier and a family tier which is preconfigured to also block adult content. A VPN takes things much further by giving you secure access to the internet via an encrypted link, hiding your address in the process and protecting you from being tracked. This also protects you when you are using public Wi-Fi hotspots as anyone snooping cannot see what you are doing. One of the antivirus companies F-Secure has a very good VPN subscription service called FREEDOME which adds additional security features and works on PCs, Macs, Apple iOS and Android devices. If you can, it's best to avoid free public Wi-Fi and make a hotspot with your mobile data instead, especially if you do not have a VPN.

4. Making sure no one else can pretend to be you is the next step, which means turning on two factor authentication (2FA) for web services you wish to protect. To get started you will need a mobile phone for basic SMS verification texts and, for more security, a smartphone using apps like

Google Authenticator. Obviously, the smartphone can handle SMS texts too. Many mainstream web services offer 2FA as a free option, you just need to turn it on and configure it. So far, I have turned on 2FA as a free option for Amazon, Apple ID, Facebook, Gmail, LinkedIn, Microsoft Outlook. com, PayPal, Twitter and Yahoo. Though, if you are prone to losing your mobile, you might want to avoid TFA. Something to be aware of if you use two factor authentication SMS texts is: if your mobile suddenly stops working and connecting to the mobile phone network displaying "emergency calls only", you may be a victim of a fraudulent SIM swap. If no one else on the same network is affected, immediately notify your bank and take your phone to the nearest mobile phone shop for your network with some ID to take back control of your phone.

5. The fifth step is to check whether you need to update any of your passwords by visiting a free website called *haveibeenpwned.com* (that's not a typo, there really is no 'a') which tells you if your email address has been compromised because a particular service has been hacked and the contents dumped online. If you have been caught in a hack or data breach, you can then change the password for the compromised account. Right now, at the time of writing, there are over 5 billion breached accounts and the list is growing. It is important to understand that from a data breach the criminals may have your name, email address, mobile, credit card number and password for that service. If you have used the same password anywhere else, you will also need to change that too. Once again, a password manager can greatly help.

6. Limiting day to day activities on a Windows computer to a user account that does not have administrator rights can stop the criminals from installing their malicious software, if you are about to be infected. Because if you aren't allowed, then chances are, they aren't either. This is known as the principle of least privilege and can help keep your computer secure. In Windows, accounts can either have full administrator rights or be standard accounts. What you want is to do all your day to day activity on a standard account, from which you are not allowed to install software. To do this you first need to create a second administrator account; you can make it the same name as your current one with admin on the end and give the account a strong password you won't forget. Once this is done, you can then remove the admin rights from your own account.

Lastly backups. I know I said six steps, but this one is a bit like insurance if the previous six steps don't work and you end up with an infection like ransomware and cannot access your files. Modern computers have lots of built-in backup features; the main thing is to have the backup somewhere else other than on or near your computer or smartphone. Copying everything onto a USB memory stick or external hard drive is great, and I recommend doing so, but a second copy in the cloud gives you increased protection. Both Apple and Google offer cloud storage for both computers and smartphones, or there are several online backup services like iDrive and Amazon Prime offers unlimited photo backup storage. Either way expect to pay something rather than try and stick to the free tiers and hopefully, like insurance, you never need it, but will be glad you have it.

There is one more thing you can do, and that is to try to do more on devices that are locked down like a Chromebook or an Apple or Android smartphone or a tablet device. If the bulk of your digital life is carried out via a tablet using apps rather than websites, you have significantly less risk than a Windows laptop user. You can still be phished, defrauded and scammed, but you will be immune to millions of malicious programs, at least until the cyber criminals change tactics.

PART 4

CYBER SECURITY ADVICE

by

CYBER AWARE

As the book out lines, it is our responsibility to take action to protect ourselves from hacking, bullying and to be cyber savvy. Some of the action needed is as simple as clicking on the privacy settings on our phone. We can all go take that extra effort to put simple security in place.

The government is a great source of information and a supporter for managing individual and business online security. CYBER AWARE (formerly Cyber Streetwise) is the government's first and only cyber security public awareness communications campaign delivering official and expert advice, based on the technical advice of the National Cyber Security Centre.

CYBER AWARE aims to make good cyber security habits second nature, not an afterthought, for individuals and small businesses. Understanding and adopting simple online security is key to enabling individuals and small businesses to become more resilient against the cyber threat while also getting the most out of being online.

People are now connected from the moment they wake up to the moment they go to sleep – creating huge opportunities to integrate positive messaging on online security into online interactions be it with family, friends, clients or employees.

The impact of a cyber breach or attack can be huge: there's the time you could lose through having to fix your website or systems, the potential loss of customers, damage to your reputation and all the other potential consequences of a hacker getting their hands on your data.

It's more important than ever to mobilise ourselves to provide this information consistently and coherently. CYBER AWARE is designed to do just this and supply key advice in the areas of,

Protecting Your Device
- Software & Apps:
  https://www.cyberaware.gov.uk/software-updates
- Security features:
  https://www.cyberaware.gov.uk/security-features

Protecting Your Data:
- Passwords:
  https://www.cyberaware.gov.uk/passwords
- Sharing Data:
  https://www.cyberaware.gov.uk/sharing-data
- Back Up data:
  https://www.cyberaware.gov.uk/back-data

Protecting Your Business:
- https://www.cyberaware.gov.uk/protect-your-business

Nearly half of all businesses, 43% reported a cyber breach or attack in the past 12 months (source: https://www.gov.uk/government/statistics/cyber-security-breaches-survey-2018).

The good news is protecting yourself from hackers and viruses does not have to take a lot of time, work or money. CYBER AWARE is encouraging the public and small businesses across the UK to do two simple things which can help improve their online security:

- Use a strong and separate password for your email (using three random words or numbers to create a strong password); hackers can use your email to access many of your personal accounts
- Install the latest software and app updates; they contain vital security updates which help protect your device from viruses and hackers

Once you put these two key actions in place, there are a range of Government-approved guidance you can follow to protect your business further.

- Cyber Essentials is an industry backed accreditation scheme for businesses, run by the Department for Culture, Digital, Media and Sport: https://www.cyberessentials.ncsc.gov.uk/
- Protect Your Data: https://ico.org.uk/for-organisations/business/
- Train Your Staff: https://www.gov.uk/government/collections/cyber-security-training-for-business
- If you are a small business and looking for more technical advice, please use the National Cyber Security Centre's Small Business Guide. https://www.ncsc.gov.uk/smallbusiness

CYBER AWARE is supported by almost 600 organisations, from law enforcement to major retailers, household brand names to charities and other Government departments, providing them with all the support and materials they need to communicate CYBER AWARE's advice in creative and innovative ways, from social media activity to co-branded advertising. We can even co-develop bespoke communications tailored to your organisation. If you would like to support the campaign, please get in touch with us at cyberaware@homeoffice.x.gsi.gov.uk.

SUMMARY

The Internet plays such an important role in our daily lives that we all need to know how best to exploit it and, at the same time, use it safely. With internet usage comes the risk of cybercrime and the risks have multiplied exponentially as we have graduated over the last 10 years from personal computers and online banking to tablets, apps and smart phones.

Whatever level of ITC skills we have attained it is impossible to achieve complete safety, but this informative book written by expert practitioners who are wise to the manifold forms of attack and intrusion practised by sophisticated cyber criminals offers recommendations how to protect yourself which everyone can use. A part of their advice includes identification of the most effective software tools that you can deploy to avoid penetration, although there are no magic bullets that will provide permanent solutions. A part of the problem is that cyber criminals are clever and innovative and no one can be sure of the nature or direction from which the next threat will come. In 2002 Donald Rumsfeld, the then US Secretary of Defense, famously noted, although not originally, that "there are things we know we know, as well as known unknowns, but that there are also unknown unknowns". The unknown unknowns are at the heart of the problems which our cybersecurity experts face continually. The best that we can do is to stay as secure as possible by following the series of simple and quickly performed reiterative actions recommended in this book.

Ultimately, good cybersecurity habits and routines should become second nature, like locking both front and back doors.

Jonathan Reuvid
Editor

CONTRIBUTORS' DETAILS

Tim Mitchell is Content Director at Get Safe Online, has responsibility for the content on the organisation's website and other awareness material, as well as its social media channels. He is a professional writer with many years' experience not only in cyber security awareness, but also writing informative and persuasive consumer and business marketing content ... and has the unusual ability to translate complex subjects into coherent, persuasive and meaningful material. Tim also represents Get Safe Online on several committees advising government and regulators about internet safety. He is a Neighbourhood Watch co-ordinator where he lives.

GET SAFE ONLINE
www.getsafeonline.org

Maureen Kendal is Director of CyberCare Ltd (cybercare.org.uk, @CyberCareUK). Cybercare offers cyber security advice and support to individuals, families, business and organisations through helplines, clinics and training workshops. Offering training to local councils, schools and communities; charities tackling social care challenges such as vulnerable adults, human trafficking and domestic abuse; police, legal and social care services.

Maureen is also an academic, educator and researcher. Previously at the Faculty of Computing and Digital Media at London Metropolitan University, she's currently a research and business associate at Ravensbourne University. She has membership and fellowships: FRSA, FHEA, MBCS, OWASP, WITT, IMIS. Maureen's business interest are within innovative immersive virtual technologies, cyber security and cyber safety.

CYBERCARE UK
www.cybercare.org.uk
Tel: 0800 211 8298
Email: maureen@cybercare.org.uk

Nick Ioannou is an IT professional, blogger and author with over 20 years' corporate experience, including 15 years using cloud/hosted software as a service (SAAS) systems. He started blogging in 2012 on free IT resources (nick-ioannou.com) currently with over 400+ posts. His first book 'Internet Security Fundamentals' available at www.booleanlogical.com, is an easy to understand guide of the most commonly faced security threats and criminal scams aimed at general users. He is also a contributing author of two Managing Cybersecurity Risk books by Legend Business Books.

BOOLEAN LOGICAL LTD
www.booleanlogical.com
Email: info@booleanlogical.com

Nick Wilding is General Manager of Cyber Resilience at AXELOS Global Best Practice, a joint company set up in 2013 and co-owned by the UK Government and

Capita plc, which owns and develops a number of best practice methodologies, including ITIL® and PRINC2®, used by organisations in more than 150 countries to enable them to work and operate more effectively. Nick is responsible for RESILIA™ Global Best Practice, a portfolio of cyber resilience best practice publications, certified training, staff awareness learning and leadership engagement tools designed to put the "human factor" at the centre of cyber resilience strategy, enabling effective recognition, response to and recovery from cyber attacks.

AXELOS RESILIA
17 Rochester Row, London SW1P 1QT
www.axelos.com/resilia
Tel: +44 (0) 207 960 7865
Email: Nick.Wilding@AXELOS.com

CYBER AWARE is a national campaign which offers advice to help the public and small businesses on how to protect themselves against the cyber threat. It is run by the Government, and the campaign advice is informed by the latest expertise from the National Cyber Security Centre.

CYBER AWARE
Tel: 020 7035 3535 (Home Office press office)
https://www.cyberaware.gov.uk
Email: cyberaware@homeoffice.x.gsi.gov.uk

Jonathan Reuvid is the editor in chief and a partner of Legend Business Books Ltd. A graduate of the University of Oxford (MA, PPE) he embarked on a second career in publishing in 1989 after a career in industry, including the role of Director of European Operations of the manufacturing divisions of a Fortune 500 multinational

and joint venture development in China. Jonathan has nearly 90 editions of more than 35 titles to his name as editor and part-author. He is a director of IPR Events London Ltd, an exhibition management company and President of the Community First Oxfordshire charity.

Legend Business Books Ltd
107-111 Fleet Street, London EC4A 2AB
Tel: 0207 936 9941
Email: jonathan.reuvid@iprevents.com

ACKNOWLEDGEMENTS

"I acknowledge the many conversations and observations of my work with my Co-director Kez Garner. With special acknowledgement and thanks going out to the research and executive teams, CyberCare consultants, trainees, our partners, professional advisors and our clients whose intelligence, courage, determination, problem-solving and compassion enables us to continue in our work. We have worked with professionals from the police, lawyers, social service, council, charity partners and communities with whom I have discussed these recurring themes and on-going challenges.

Thanks to Danny Allen, who has patiently proof read and discussed the finer points of this chapter.

Lastly, a heartfelt thanks to my family for their inspiration, warmth, love and unwavering support."

Maureen Kendal

"Legend Business expresses their grateful thanks to the authors who have written and without whose contributions this book could not be published. Their further advice is available to all readers and listed within the contributors page. Thanks also to Liza Paderes for managing as well as developing the content and schedule, to Ditte Løkkegaard for ensuring the book is typeset and printed to the highest standard and to Jonathan Reuvid who edited the text of these key industry authors."

Legend Business

MORE CYBER BOOKS BY LEGEND BUSINESS

MANAGING CYBERSECURITY RISK: BOOK 1
How to protect your business
ISBN: 9781785079153
£39.99

MANAGING CYBERSECURITY RISK: BOOK 2
Case Studies and Solutions
ISBN: 9781787198913
£39.99

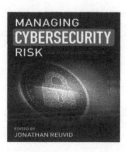